MARE TARTARICUM

ASIA

OCEANUS OCCIDENTALIS

AUSTRALIA

LEPIDOPTERA →

THE DISTRIBUTION
OF BUTTERFLIES AND MOTHS

As illustrated on endpaper maps

---

1 ARGYNNIS – Europe, Asia and North America

2 COLIAS – Europe, Asia and North America

3 VANESSA URTICAE – Europe and Northern Asia

4 VANESSA IO – Europe and Northern Asia

5 VANESSA ANTIOPA – Europe, Northern Asia, North America

6 PIERIS – Europe, Asia, Africa, America

7 PAPILIO MACHAON – Europe and Northern Asia

8 SATURNIA PYRI – Southern Europe

9 PARNASSIUS APOLLO – Europe

10 PARNASSIUS AUTOCRATOR – Hindu Kush

11 GRAELLSIA ISABELLAE – Spain

12 BOMBYX MORI – China

13 ACTIAS SELENE – India

14 ANTHERAEA PERNYI – China

15 ANTHERAEA YAMAMAI – Japan

16 ATTACUS ATLAS – India

17 ATTACUS JAVANUS – Java

18 ATTACUS CAESAR – Philippines (Mindanao)

19 ORNITHOPTERA TROJANUS – Philippines (Palawan)

20 ORNITHOPTERA BROOKIANA – Sumatra, Borneo

21 ORNITHOPTERA PARADISEA – New Guinea

22 ORNITHOPTERA LYDIUS – Halmahera

23 ORNITHOPTERA HECUBA – Key Island

24 SPHINGIDAE – World-wide

25 DRURYA ANTIMACHUS – Central Africa

26 PAPILIO ZALMOXIS – Central Africa

27 LOBOBUNEA – Central Africa

28 URANIA CROESUS – East Africa

29 ARGEMA MIMOSAE – Central Africa

30 ARGEMA MITTREI – Madagascar

31 URANIA RIPHEUS – Madagascar

32 PAPILIO ANTENOR – Madagascar

33 ACTIAS LUNA – North America

34 PLATYSAMIA CECROPIA – North America

35 PAPILIO HOMERUS – Jamaica

36 MORPHO – Bolivia, Brazil, Peru, Colombia

37 AGRIAS – South America

38 PREPONA – South America

39 SPHINGIDAE – South America

40 COPIOPTERYX SEMIRAMIS – Venezuela and Northern Brazil

41 HELICONIUS – South America

BUTTERFLIES AND MOTHS

BUTTERFLIES AND MOTHS

REVISED EDITION

Norman Riley, Editor

Text by Alfred Werner and Josef Bijok

A Studio Book · THE VIKING PRESS · New York

FLIEGENDE KLEINODIEN

© SCHULER VERLAG STUTTGART 1955

REVISED AND ENLARGED EDITION PUBLISHED IN 1965
BY THE VIKING PRESS, INC.
625 MADISON AVENUE, NEW YORK, N.Y. 10022

REISSUED IN 1970 WITH FURTHER REVISIONS AND ADDITIONS
SBN 670-19782-3

LIBRARY OF CONGRESS CATALOG CARD NUMBER: 65-15377

PRINTED IN GERMANY
BY K.G. LOHSE FRANKFURT-AM-MAIN

BOUND IN GERMANY

Frontispiece:
Microphotograph of part of the hind wing of
Chrysiridia madagascariensis (Urania ripheus)
See also Plate 32.

CONTENTS

Plato argued that poets, as a dangerous class, should be barred from the ideal commonwealth he described in his *Republic*. There are many who would not mind seeing the Lepidoptera — butterflies and moths — barred from this earth. The butterflies that have moved poets to write soaring lyrics are cursed by the farmer for the millions of eggs they lay on artichokes, cabbages and cauliflowers, eggs from which will inevitably emerge millions of voracious caterpillars. Many a housewife feels equally vindictive about the clothes moth, which is a menace to her carpets and woollens.

There are insects that are indefatigable and useful workers. Besides the bees, which produce wax and honey, and which, like the ants, are excellent administrators, there are, among the insects, carpenters, spinners, weavers, miners, fishermen, musicians, garbage collectors, and so on. Yet some butterflies and moths are very useful, too, at least from man's point of view.

Even a housewife will forgive moths if she remembers that the silkworm has rendered an incomparable service to man for nearly five thousand years by yielding twelve pounds of raw silk for every ounce of eggs. The stern men who wrote the Bible failed to mention butterflies, and referred to moths as evil things. But is it not enough that these insects, or quite a number of them, are a delight to behold? What of the lilies of the field? Besides, the Lepidoptera, and in particular the butterflies, are far less idle, less carefree than they have generally been thought to be.

Lepidoptera are, next to bees, the most efficient pollenizers. Nature stores nectar in flowers in such a way that insects wishing to reach it must come into contact with the flower's reproductive organs. Being sticky, the pollen adheres to the body of the visiting insect, which dislocates and relocates it as it moves. During the day it is butterflies, at night moths, that keep busy transferring the pollen from the androecium to the gynoecium, from the male to the female.

Many a layman is prejudiced against bugs which appear to him to be unworthy of any serious study — even the marvellous creatures whose likenesses are shown in this book. Fortunately, others feel differently. And it is for them that the many fascinating volumes on butterflies and moths of the temperate zone have been written. Yet little has been written in English on the Lepidoptera of the tropics, and virtually all those of the species shown in these pages belong to this category.

Here are a few facts concerning these insects, of which two hundred and twenty thousand different kinds have been counted: about one hundred and seventy-five thousand moths, the remainder butterflies. In learned circles, the order is called *Lepidoptera* (singular, *Lepidopteron*), a name given them by that eighteenth-century Swedish genius, Linnaeus, the father of natural history, who originated the binominal system (genus and species) for designating plants and animals. The word *Lepidoptera* was coined by combining the Greek words for scale and wing (four scaled wings being the characteristic of nearly all butterflies and moths). The technical term for one of the two sub-orders, the butterflies, is *Rhopalocera*, from the Greek words for club and horn, referring to the fact that the butterfly's antennae or feelers, usually long and slender, end in a little knob which sometimes has a short apiculus. The term for the moths, *Heterocea*, is less graphic; it comes from the Greek words for other and horn, and thus defines the moths as Lepidoptera whose antennae are other than club-shaped. The many forms the antennae take are described below (p. 38). Although butterflies and moths are cousins, there are several differences between them. Some of these are of greater concern to the entomologist, who studies all the life stages, than to the layman, who is primarily interested in the perfect adult insect (the imago). For instance, the pupa or chrysalis of the butterfly is seldom enclosed in any form of cocoon. Many moths, and especially the silkworm, construct very strong and closely woven coverings, the so-called cocoons. The eyes of the butterflies are usually much larger and more prominent than those of moths—but minute and careful examination of the individual insects is required in order to observe this.

There are simpler differences that are also easier to remember. While at rest, butterflies fold their wings vertically over their heads, whereas moths hold theirs horizontally, so that they look like grounded aeroplanes. The most important difference, however, is in their living habits: the great majority of butterflies are diurnal; they fly only between sunrise and dusk. Most moths, on the other hand, are nocturnal; they fly only by night, or in the twilight before dawn. Moths, with the exception of clothes moths, are known for their tendency to fly towards light, and can often be seen whirling around light beacons. Thoreau tells of moths covering the window of a beacon on Cape Cod in such immense numbers as to endanger the lives of mariners by dimming the rays from the lighthouse. Butterflies, however, are great lovers of sunlight: when a cloud suddenly obscures it, many go to rest. In a temperate climate, butterflies reach their peak of activity about midday. They do not like cool overcast days, but happily take to wing as soon as the faintest rays from the sun pierce the clouds.

However, there are some diurnal moths as well. In fact, talking about the habits of Lepidoptera is as hazardous as speaking about the rules of grammar in any language — there are too many exceptions. There are so many varieties, so many conflicting data; so many 'facts' that have been scrapped by naturalists, and so many answers to puzzling phenomena that are still in the hypothetical stage — that there is enough work for generations of scientists to come.

This may sound surprising, if we consider that both Aristotle and Pliny gave much attention to the Lepidoptera. Significantly, many of the false notions developed in antiquity about these insects proved almost indestructible. For instance, Izaak Walton repeats unquestioningly information he had obtained from Gaius Plinius Secundus, a contemporary of the Emperor Nero. Walton, who loved to watch the butterflies and caterpillars on the banks of the streams he fished, wrote with disarming naïvety:

'Pliny holds an opinion, that many caterpillars have their birth, or being, from a dew that in the spring falls upon the leaves of trees.'

Centuries earlier, one of the most learned men of the Middle Ages, the Dominican Albertus Magnus, a teacher of St Thomas Aquinas, considered caterpillars (which he supposed laid eggs!) and butterflies ('winged worms of various colour') entirely unrelated.

Today we know vastly more about insects than Aristotle, who used to watch the caterpillars of the white butterflies devouring his cabbage, or Pliny, who is said to have set up a mare's skull as a 'scare-butterfly' in his cabbage patch. Both Albertus Magnus and Izaak Walton would be overwhelmed even by the knowledge concerning insects contained nowadays in a high school text book. The compound microscope has helped us to see clearly details that no lens of the past could reveal, and we obtain further aid through micro-photography and the application of x-rays. Yet the field of entomology has expanded so much in recent decades that no one can possibly hope to understand and survey with equal authority all of the thirty-four orders into which the seven hundred and fifty thousand kinds of insects have been classified. Oliver Wendell Holmes, who more than eigthy years ago watched the beginnings of modern natural science, wrote the following exchange in *The Poet at the Breakfast Table:* 'I suppose you are an entomologist?'

'Not quite so ambitious as that, Sir . . . No man can be truly called an entomologist, Sir: the subject is too vast for any single human intelligence to grasp.'

Lepidoptera existed long before Man. Although their delicacy prevented their common preservation as fossils, fossilized remains of Lepidoptera have been found in Europe and America which are closely related to species of the present day. Some of them seem to have been rather large, though not as big as is generally believed. The largest insect, not a Lepidopteron, was a forerunner of our dragonflies and had a wingspread of two feet, or barely twice that of the largest butterflies and moths existing today. Lepidoptera can be found in all but the coldest parts of the world, and everywhere their basic physical structure is the same.

The body of the perfect imago (adult insect) consists — like ancient Gaul — of three parts: the head, the thorax, and the abdomen. Curiously, it has no mouth parts on the head other than a long hollow tongue which it can extend to draw up liquid nourishment, pumping honeyed moisture out of the blossoms, or sipping much less poetic fluids from garbage and dung. Let us remember that Lepidoptera do damage only in the caterpillar stage when they have very efficient chewing equipment to feed their vigorous appetites, and can destroy the contents of our cupboards or the crops of field and forest with amazing speed.

On either side of the head is a large globular compound eye consisting of thousands of minute hexagonal facets, each registering an image (the Swallowtail is credited with thirty-four thousand of these facets). Of vital importance are the antennae, enabling the insect to smell, to communicate with others of its kind, and to maintain its balance — without them it cannot fly.

There are three pairs of legs on the thorax but the first pair are not always fully developed. Oddly enough, some butterflies seem to have a sense of taste in the rear pair of legs, for as soon as these touch a sweet substance, the insect uncoils its tongue to drink (butterflies apparently have a sharp 'sweet tooth': they can detect sugar in a mixture of one part to three hundred thousand, whereas we poor humans can detect sweetness only where there is at least one part sugar in two hundred).

I shall discuss the wings of Lepidoptera in a separate chapter. Let us consider first the state of Lepidoptera when they have no wings. Martin Luther, though he may have known of the metamorphoses the butterflies and their cousins undergo, spoke of the caterpillar as 'an emblem of the Devil in its crawling walk', and, inversely, the poet, John Gay, two hundred years later, decried the butterfly, which was 'at best... but a caterpillar, drest'.

One cannot blame those of an earlier day who saw no connection between the flying gems they watched fluttering from flower to flower, and the ugly little beast preoccupied with eating up leaf after leaf. The difference between the common butterfly, such as the Brimstone (from whose colour the Anglo-Saxons derived the name *butterfleoge*), and its caterpillar is great enough, yet it is almost beyond our capacity to envisage that even the proud Papilios of the tropics were 'first grubs obscene, then wriggling worms', to use Pope's drastic description, before reaching their full glory. But this is democracy in the truest sense, democracy in the animal kingdom—which prescribes the same, or nearly the same, life and death for the most glamorous as well as for the most inconspicuous members of an insect order.

Our anthropomorphic attitude towards animals often blinds us to a real understanding of the facts of nature. For instance, we think of butterflies as blissfully happy in an eternal search for pleasure. The truth is that these apparently carefree creatures are unbelievably busy propagating their race. Any nature student can explode the notion that butterflies are merely dainty ornaments of garden, field, and woods, flitting about and sipping nectar from flowers. The burden of their work falls to the female—the male plays second fiddle in the insect world. After mating, she must find a place for the eggs she produces, each no larger than a drop of dew. On a sunny day, a female may cover a great many miles in her search for the proper food-plants, or, in the case of clothes moths, which undergo analogous metamorphoses, for fabrics and furs. She can deposit as many as a hundred eggs in an hour. A wonderful instinct tells her which plant will best suit the development of the larvae, for the caterpillar when it is hatched, after from two to thirty days' incubation of the many-shaped eggs, will live on, and nourish itself from, this same plant.

Hatched by the warmth of the sun, the caterpillar breaks through the envelope of the egg shell. Whereas a grasshopper, just hatched from the egg, is very like his father and mother, the caterpillar has not the slightest resemblance to either. It is this and the sequent metamorphosis that caused two mid-nineteenth-century authors of a textbook thus to voice their bewilderment:

'Were a naturalist to announce to the world the discovery of an animal which first existed in the form of a serpent; which then . . . weaving a shroud of pure silk of the finest texture, contracted itself within this covering into a body without external mouth or limbs, and resembling, more than anything else, an Egyptian mummy and which, lastly, after remaining in this state without food and without motion . . . should at the end of that period burst its silken cerements, struggle through its earthly covering and start into day a winged bird—what think you would be the sensation excited by this strange piece of intelligence? After the first doubts of its truth were dispelled, what astonishment would succeed! Among the learned, what surmises!—what investigations! Even the most torpid would flock to the sight of such a prodigy!'

To get back to the caterpillar, its first and only activity is—to eat. It is calculated that within twenty-four hours it consumes more than twice its own weight in food, and that within a month it increases to nearly ten thousand times its original weight. In the course of weeks, the skin is cast off several times, and eventually the next stage is reached, that of a pupa (differing in shape and size among butterflies and moths). For a couple of weeks or so the insect remains in the chrysalis. This is exposed but secured by a silken girdle or attached to a pad, while many moths weave themselves tightly closed cocoons. No nourishment, of course, is taken during this stationary period, yet in the 'cage' the insect is growing and changing into a winged being, the imago. On the day the skin of the chrysalis splits, the butterfly, or moth, still wet, weak and undecided, but perfect, emerges from the shell. There is no further growth — moths and butterflies do not appear in their winged insecthood until they are in the final phase of their development, and when they have reached it they do no more growing or changing.

We could continue with dozens of episodes from the Lepidopteron's life, but we shall instead point to two phenomena that may puzzle the reader: dimorphism — the existence of two distinct forms in the same species; and polymorphism — the similar existence of several forms. Males of a species frequently wear different garments, usually lighter and brighter than those of the females: often there are also differences in size, and in some cases the female may be the larger (sexual dimorphism). There may be marked differences between those insects of a species which appear in the spring, having passed their chrysalis stage under the snow, and the broods of summer and autumn, or, in the tropics, between the creatures of the hot season, and those of the dry season (seasonal dimorphism and polymorphism). Often these two or three kinds of differences are so marked that naturalists believed they were faced with separate species — until further research and more careful observation revealed the true relationships.

A large number of insects possess wings, as is indicated by the Greek names given to such orders as Orthoptera (among which are the locusts), Dermaptera (earwigs), Plecoptera (stoneflies), and so on. Yet not a single one of these can boast wings as large and as beautiful as those of some of the Lepidoptera. Their soul, their very existence, is in their wings. How insignificant would they be without them! The butterflies, in particular, have disproportionally large wings: the body-weight of a medium-sized butterfly may be roughly that of a large bee, yet the wing expanse is twenty times that of a bee of equal weight. If these wings should be broken off — because the insect has been dashed by a strong wind against something hard, or an attacker has managed to bite them off — the little creature is doomed to perish. Even if too many of the scales are rubbed off the insect's life will be radically shortened, for scales that are lost are not replaced by new growth; in the first place, the protective colour has become imperfect, and the insect is now more likely to be spotted by greedy enemies; secondly, its ability to fly is hampered both by the displacement of weight (in the healthy insect, the wings on one side are perfectly balanced by those on the other) and by the uneven flow of air over the wing's surface. With awkward and halting flight, it can no longer elude the swift birds that prey upon it.

As children, nearly all of us got 'butterfly dust' on our fingers, whether we systematically hunted these lovely creatures in gardens and fields in order to collect them, or whether, in a mischievous mood, we simply caught one or two. But adults are more apt to appreciate the insect's fragile and brittle charm; as we grow older, most of us come to deplore wanton or careless destruction.

The naturalist is not guilty on this score, but he cannot afford to be sentimental, either. For hundreds of years he has been hunting, killing and mounting Lepidoptera for the sake of thorough study, and millions of specimens can be admired in museums all over the world and in the collections of the great universities. The samples range from the very tiny and inconspicuous to the real marvels of nature. The tiniest Lepidopteron is probably the Golden Pigmy of Great Britain, a moth whose wings are only one fifth of an inch across. The title of the largest Lepidopteron is claimed by the huge bat-like Atlas moth *(Attacus atlas)* of India), said to be the biggest flying insect in the world, with a wingspread of about a foot; if reproduced in its actual size, it would more than cover a full page of this book. Only a little smaller is that gorgeous bird-wing butterfly, *Papilio alexandrae,* of New Guinea, with a wing expanse of over ten inches.

Seen under a microscope, however, even the smallest wing offers a world of unmatched excitement. The scales, of varying sizes and intricate shapes, are held in place by a stem fitted into a pocket in the chitin, the horny skin. There is no difference between these scales and those covering the insect's body, which usually have the same colours, but often have some extra touches added to the head, thorax, and abdomen.

The magnifying lens reveals an arrangement resembling that of shingles on a roof. On most roofs, however, only one colour is used, whereas on a Lepidopteron's wing there is an endless diversity of colouring, with enough different patterns and designs to put the inventive minds of Persian carpetmakers to shame. We admire a painter like Seurat for having produced every possible shade of colour by means of a great many tiny dots of equal size spread over a canvas like confetti. Yet how poor this accomplishment is compared to that of the Master who painted the wings of a Brazilian Morpho (*morpho,* a Greek term, means 'shapely'). He placed one hundred and sixty-five rows of scales, with six hundred scales in each row, on every square inch of the wing. This makes no fewer than ninety-nine thousand scales to a square inch, with the total number of scales on fifteen square inches of wing surface approaching a million and a half.

There is no need to describe or further to extol the adornments of the Lepidopteron's wings — the lovely colour plates in this volume will speak for themselves. But it is interesting to know how this richness of colour is produced. There are pigmental and structural colours. The former are genuine pigments, like the dyes that colour a dress, and these are responsible for the blacks, browns, yellows and dull reds on a wing. When, with the insect's death, the cells die, the colour preserved in the chitin of the scales remains, even though it may fade in course of time.

The structural colours, however — such as the iridescent metallic blues and greens — are imperishable, for they are caused by the fragmentation of the spectrum reflected or absorbed by the minute grooves and other tiny structures in the scales. One might compare them to the colours produced by a glass prism. Take the gleaming blue of the Brazilian Morpho: it is caused by light broken up and reflected into such intricate forms that only the most intense blue rays reach the eye, while all other rays are eliminated. The scales are so constructed that they reflect light rays of a certain wave length, whereas the others pass through them. In general, it can be said that the over-all colour pattern that we see is due to the effects of light, either by

CHRYSIRIDIA MADAGASCARIENSIS
LESS
Uraniidae
Distribution: *Madagascar*
Caterpillar feeds on Euphorbiaceae

PAPILIO SARPEDON TEREDON FLDR
Papilionidae Swallowtails
Distribution: *Southern India, Ceylon*

PRECIS ORITHYA L.
Nymphalidae
Distribution: *China*

PAPILIO ALCINOUS LOOCHOOANUS
ROTHSCH
Papilionidae Swallowtails
Distribution: *Loo-Choo (Ryukyu Islands)*

absorption or by reflection. At the same time, the most striking effects are produced by the interplay of both structural and pigmental colours.

There are also Lepidoptera whose wings have no scales, and might be compared to transparent windows, with the delicate glass-like surface showing only a network of tender veins. Such 'transparent' butterflies are to be found in the Andean jungle of Colombia. In flight they are easily seen, but on coming to rest among brown leaves which cover the forest floor, they become more or less invisible. If their wings are placed upon a printed page, one may read through these wings as readily as through a piece of glass.

This same optical phenomenon will cause a butterfly's iridescent or metallic colours to change when viewed from different angles. If you rub some scales from a wing — they are so lightly attached that the gentlest touch will remove thousands at once — and put them on a glass slide under a microscope, thus allowing the light to shine through them from the mirror below, you will find them neither blue nor green, but either containing a brownish pigment or entirely empty and transparent.

Sometimes nature seems to be playful and embroiders little jokes on a Lepidopteron's wing. China's Map butterfly, one of the Nymphalidae, received its name from the fact that its wings are adorned with brown and white markings that make them look like a page from a geography book. A genus of butterflies in Latin America is called Catagramma, from the Greek for 'a letter beneath', with reference to the curious markings on the underside of their wings which resemble Arabic numerals. *Catagramma kolyma*, for instance, carries the number '88'. In the case of the Death's-Head moth, *Acherontia atropos*, whose habitat is Northern Africa and Southern Europe, the ornament, a threatening skull, is not on the wings, but on the back of the thorax. *Papilio priamus* has an abdomen that looks as if it were of gold.

It should be understood that even the most perfectly preserved specimens of butterflies and moths in our museum collections do not retain all of the overpowering glamour shown by the living insect in its natural habitat, especially the tropical Lepidopteron in its jungle, when the pigmental colours are freshly alive, while the iridescent overlay is produced by vivid shafts of light falling on and reflected from the closely set series of ridges and grooves.

On the whole, however, butterflies, being children of the sun, fade only little after death, and this also applies to day-flying moths. Moths which hide during the day and fly only in darkness have pigments ill adapted for exposure, and the colours of their wings are bound to fade behind glass. Collectors are, therefore, warned that moths must be kept in dark cabinets. In even a single season the colours of a collection of moths, particularly the larger specimens, will, if exposed to strong light, fade to the extent of ruining the insects' glamour.

Even matter-of-fact naturalists who have collected, described, and classified hundreds or thousands of Lepidoptera have been unable to resist the magic charm of these creatures. Thus a contemporary American naturalist, Donald Culross Peattie, writes:

'Upon the slim, six-legged body of the insect, nature, like a madly inspired couturière, has tried thousands of fabulous colours and cuts and patterns. Man with all his looms and dyes cannot create anything half so exquisite as a butterfly's wing.'

And on another occasion, the same author writes:

'The beauty of a butterfly's wing, the beauty of all things, is not a slave to purpose, a drudge sold to futurity. It is excrescence, superabundance, random ebullience, and sheer waste to be enjoyed in its own high rights.'

THE IMPORTANCE OF APPEARANCE

Hobbes in his *Leviathan* pointed out that originally, before governments were established by men, all behaviour was dictated exclusively by motives of self-preservation, and that in this primitive state force and fraud were the two cardinal virtues in the continual war of all against all. How far Man has succeeded in subduing his starkly selfish instincts by application of religious or political principles is difficult to say, and the pessimist's view will, of course, minimize the extent to which civilization has mitigated or transformed our egotistical instincts. Certainly, in the animal kingdom, the ruthless war of all against all goes on with the same fierceness as in the Stone Age. Whether we speak with Herbert Spencer of the 'survival of the fittest', or with Charles Darwin of 'natural selection', both expressions refer to the rule of the lawless jungle, which gives the right to live only to those who manage to avoid being eaten by others.

The enemies of the Lepidoptera are legion. Being among the weakest creatures in the animal world they can exert little force and have to resort to 'fraud' in order to survive. Among those who prey on them there is, of course, Man with his hunting net, Man who, with insecticides, kills millions by destroying them before they have taken wing. Perhaps nature did not provide for Man as a potential enemy of these insects when, at the dawn of history, he appeared on the stage as a not particularly dangerous animal—except for his expanding and increasingly inventive brain. But nature protected the Lepidoptera from the many other assailants, particularly numerous in the tropical lands, ranging from monkeys, birds and bats to snakes, lizards and spiders. To elude these, the Lepidoptera needed wings—yet some of their enemies also can fly, and fly faster.

Studying the 'wiles' that have enabled the Lepidoptera to deceive their foes, the naturalists have observed two special defences, 'Protective Resemblance' and 'Mimicry'. It goes without saying that the former—achieving concealment through a likeness to an object of no interest to enemies—as well as the latter—advantageous resemblances between animals—occurs among mammals, birds, reptiles and fishes, and even in the plant world. But the best illustrations of the operation of these devices, which contribute to the preservation of certain species, can be noted among butterflies and moths.

These insects use 'camouflage' for the same reason as Man uses it in warfare — as disguise for the purpose of making a vulnerable object melt into its surroundings. But while armies have to resort to artificial aids such as paints and nettings in order to screen gun installations and vital buildings, butterflies and moths are equipped by nature with all they need for camouflage. That portion of their wings which is exposed while they rest on rocks, tree trunks, or leaves — in the case of butterflies the underside, in that of moths the upper side — is much less conspicuously coloured than the glorious wing-surfaces displayed in the course of flight. This dull brown or green facing is so like the object on which the insect perches that, although fully exposed to view, it can only be detected through the closest scrutiny. Often special shadings of the insect reduce the sharpness of outline and the conspicuous play of shadows. But nature goes even further: butterflies tilt their wings at such an angle as not only to make the most of the concealing colouration, but even to minimize, or perhaps to avoid completely, whatever treacherous shadows might betray the insect's whereabouts.

The most dramatic example of protective resemblance is offered by the beautiful Kallima butterfly of the East Indies. Its large wings are ornamented on the uppermost surface with blue and orange patches, making the insect very conspicuous in flight. While flying it is able to escape capture by birds, hence these bright colours are not a disadvantage. But when it settles on a twig, it can enjoy its well-deserved rest without fear, for it seems to disappear as though by a trick of magic. All it does is to come to rest with its head up and its wings folded together over its back, exposing the brownish dead-leaf-like undersurface which makes it look like a decayed leaf still clinging to the parent stem. Alfred Russel Wallace, the eminent British naturalist, who pursued this scintillating and evasive insect through the jungles of the Malay Archipelago, wrote about his hunting expedition:

'I often endeavoured to capture it without success, for after flying a short distance it would enter a bush among dry or dead leaves, and however carefully I crept up to the spot I could never discover it till it would suddenly start out again and then disappear in a similar place. At length I was fortunate enough to see the exact spot where the butterfly settled, and though I lost sight of it for some time, I at length discovered that it was close before my eyes, but that in its position of repose it so closely resembled a dead leaf attached to a twig, as almost certainly to deceive the eye even when gazing full upon it.'

A similar story was told more recently by the American, William Beebe, who watched several Heliconiid butterflies of South America asleep three feet above ground:

'At perfect eye focus they merged completely with their surroundings, being blackish brown with a few

20

ACRAEA ONCAEA HPFF.
Nymphalidae
Distribution: *South and East Africa as far as the Congo, Abyssinia*

CATOPSILIA FLORELLA FABR.
Pieridae Whites
Distribution: *Asia, China, India, Ceylon, Persia, tropical Africa*

PSEUDACRAEA DOLOMENA
ALBOSTRIATA LATHY
Nymphalidae
Distribution: *Uganda*

PAPILIO ANACTUS MAC LEAY
Papilionidae Swallowtails
Distribution: *Northern Queensland to New South Wales*
Caterpillar feeds on Ruta and Citrus

solid and dotted bands of creamy buff. The dark parts simply did not exist, and this left the bands hanging in space, mere continuation of the maze of pale, dead, angled twigs which stretched in every direction.'

Beebe also reported from the Venezuelan Andes an interesting case of a native butterfly that manages to elude his enemies by dazzling and confusing them:

'The fore wings were plain dark brown, as was the visible part of the hinder when partly covered. A forward push of the front ones revealed a great central splash of iridescent morpho blue, bordered at a distance with a galactic curve of eight pigment hues, each with an upper and lower lid of amber, and made alive by a brilliant spark of iridescent green. When, in flight, the fore wings were suddenly spread and raised, the effect in sunlight was of an electric light suddenly flashed spang into one's eyes. The result gave a good chance at escape, whether from lizard, monkey, bird, or man.'

The Lepidoptera have developed tricks beyond those of Protective Resemblance. It is still uncertain whether certain large spots on wings are 'designed' to frighten enemies (possibly because of some resemblance to owls or snakes) or whether they merely serve as 'lightning rods' for the assailant's attack. For even if a hole is pierced in a wing, the insect can still fly well enough to escape, whereas an attack on the body would mutilate it and put it out of action. It seems, then, that nature provided many Lepidoptera with enormous wings in order to distract attention from more vital spots. Jungle explorers have seen specimens surviving with pierced and broken wings; often with only the 'swallow tails' — more conspicuously coloured than the main body of wings — destroyed.

Earlier, we mentioned insects protected by the 'transparency' of their wings. Some butterflies so closely resemble flowers that they are hard to discern. Seasonal dimorphism also plays a role: since in the tropics the battle for survival is less severe in the wet season, insects born during it are in less need of protective colours than members of the same species who have the misfortune of struggling for existence during the dry season.

'Mimicry of death' (not confined to the Lepidoptera, since it can also be found among beetles, bugs and other insects) does not really belong in a chapter on Mimicry. It is not agreed among naturalists whether it is an act of instinctive shamming — 'feigning' death — or whether the enemy's touch produces a physiological state resembling *rigor mortis*. Much has been written on Mimicry in the strict sense of the term which is often, and always erroneously, lumped together with Protective Resemblance. For Mimicry implies that one defenceless animal imitates, not a static object, vegetable or mineral, but another active animal that is not attractive to potential predators and, therefore, not likely to be attacked. Mimicry is not confined to any particular zone. In the northern latitudes a butterfly called the Viceroy is immune to attack because it looks like the inedible Monarch. One of the hawk moths even looks like a large and dangerous hornet.

Many examples can be found in the tropics. There are many Papilios that fly very slowly and dangerously close to the ground. Surprisingly, the fact that they can very easily be spotted by insectivorous animals is, in this particular case, an advantage: by flaunting certain gaudy hues (termed 'warning colours' by Alfred Russel Wallace), these clever strategists advertise in unmistakable terms the fact that they have an offensive taste.

But this is only the beginning of the story. The great British naturalist, Henry Walter Bates, who studied the phenomena of Mimicry in the South American jungles, noted that some Heliconiidae, inedible and thus immune from attacks by animals, are 'copied' by edible Pieridae. In other words, the latter so closely resemble the lucky Heliconiidae that they are almost indistinguishable and are therefore also shunned by birds and other enemies.

To understand what is called 'Batesian Mimicry' one must bear in mind that insects like these Pieridae did not, of course, make any conscious effort to 'mimic' the 'model', to assume the form and colour of the Heliconiidae. Why nature works that way, no man can tell, but Wallace found a simple and convincing explanation:

'The number of species of insects is so great, and there is such diversity of form and proportion in every group, that the chances of an accidental approximation in size, form, and colour of one insect to another of a different group is considerable; and it is these chance approximations that furnish the basis of mimicry, to be continually advanced and perfected by the survival of those varieties only which tend in the right direction.'

But there was another phenomenon of the jungle waiting for a satisfactory explanation: 'distasteful' species have a tendency to resemble each other. It was a German naturalist living in Brazil, Fritz Mueller, who proposed an explanation. According to 'Muellerian Mimicry' the common colouration helps to 'educate' the enemies. Young insectivorous creatures, not yet knowing what they may or may not eat, are apt to attack inedible insects, but will, after several disappointments, refrain from repeating the same error. Since several species sport the same warning colouration, the relative loss which each of them suffers through such misguided assaults will be bearable for each of them — thanks to the common trademark. Muellerian Mimicry

24

thus turns out to be of advantage to everyone concerned. E. B. Poulton cleverly characterized the difference between the two theories thus:

'A Batesian mimic may be compared to an unscrupulous tradesman who copies the advertisement of a successful firm; Muellerian mimicry, to a combination between firms to adopt a common advertisement and share the expenses.'

It goes without saying that interpolation of motives taken from human behaviour to the animal world can lead to misconceptions such as that, in order to be left alone by would-be-enemies, the palatable 'mimic' resorts to a life of deception. This must be understood only in a metaphoric sense. What can be said is that the sham warning colouration functions to ward off enemies who mistake the mimic for the model, since they know from previous experience that the model is not 'good eating'.

THE TRAVELLER

Mass movements or changes of habitat occur frequently among animals. Everyone is familiar with the periodic migrations of birds which breed in the north in the summer but spend the winters in the milder atmosphere of countries farther to the south. Less widely known, because they are less widely observed, are the migrations of salmon, eels, reindeer, or the Alaska fur seals, and that some butterflies travel extensively will surprise many people.

The travels of such delicate creatures over hundreds or even thousands of miles of land or sea is almost incredible. Indeed, most butterflies and moths are not at all travel-minded. Living a short life of one to three weeks, they flutter around and die within a relatively small area, perhaps the same garden in which they first emerged from the pupa. But there are some species that equal some of the most enterprising mammals and birds in the extent of their flight. There is one basic difference between the migrations of the higher animals and those of Lepidoptera. The former have longer lives, and the individual usually journeys more than once in each direction. In the insect world, where the life span is rarely longer than ten months or perhaps a year, the 'round trip' is usually completed, not by the same individual, but by the second or third generation.

Mass flights of butterflies were already recorded in Europe during the Middle Ages. Columbus saw great flocks of butterflies off the coast of Cuba being dispersed by a tropical storm. The Thistle butterfly, or Painted Lady *(Vanessa cardui)* of the Old World, one of the commonest and most cosmopolitan of butterflies, spends the winter in the North African desert and in the early spring crosses the Mediterranean to move northward across Europe. A few members of this species are known to have reached Northern Russia, Scandinavia, Scotland, and even Iceland, and thus to have flown well over a thousand miles. In 1879 the Painted Lady came out of Africa 'in clouds that cast shadows on the grounds'. Darwin, in *Zoology of the Voyage of H.M.S. Beagle,* reported that when travelling on the vessel off the coast of South America he saw vast numbers of butterflies in bands, or flocks, in countless myriads as far as the eye could see, 'so that it was not possible to see the space above the snowing butterflies'. He remarked that the column, flying six hundred feet above the ocean, was a mile wide, and he believed it to be many miles long.

26

TAJURIA JALINDRA HSF
Lycaenidae Blues
Distribution: *India*

DENDORIX HEW
Lycaenidae Blues
Distribution: *Batjan Island, Australia*

RAHINDA VIRAJA FRUHST
Nymphalidae
Distribution: *India*

NEPTIS MINDORANA ILOCANA FELD
Nymphalidae
Distribution: *Northern Philippines*

More recently, William Beebe watched a butterfly migration in Venezuela:

'As far as I could tell, the density was quite unaffected by altitude. The closer the butterflies flew to the stars, the more astronomical became their number. For days the same migration kept up, millions upon untold millions coming from some unknown sources, travelling to an equally mysterious destination. Here, on my little mound in the heart of the Venezuelan Andes, my mind recalled a phrase uttered by a Roman gentleman named Cicero, two thousand years ago, concerning "the insatiable variety of nature".'

The caterpillars of the Painted Lady kill the artichokes of the farmers on the Riviera and the tobacco plants of the settlers in the Holy Land, while the periodic northward movement of the Cotton worm *(Alabama argillacea)* from its habitat in South or Central America is dreaded by the cotton growers of the Carolinas, Georgia, Alabama, and other Southern states.

However, the most fascinating of all travellers among the Lepidoptera, the Monarch or Wanderer *(Danaus plexippus)*, is not considered a pest, for its caterpillars thrive on milkweeds, common plants of no value to man. (On account of this preference, the insect is also called the Milkweed butterfly.)

One of the largest butterflies of America, the Monarch is also one of the most common, and not especially distinguished for its attractiveness. Still, this orange, black and white butterfly is different from the others, those contented stay-at-homes so utterly devoid of 'curiosity'. Is it over-population and the reduction in food plants for caterpillars that drives them to engage in what the entomologist Edwin Way Teale called 'one of the strangest mass movements in the insect world'? Or is it the climate that influences the Monarch's southward migration in the autumn and 'return' migration in the spring? It is known that the majority of insects are killed as soon as their tissues freeze; in other words, the fall of the mercury brings them death. Perhaps 'hunger' and cold are the principal driving factors.

Only an outline of the fascinating tale can be given here. On the approach of cold weather the Monarchs of Canada and the northern United States congregate in immense numbers, just as birds do when they get ready for their migration. There may be thousands of butterflies in a swarm. In the morning, when they arise at a given signal (about which nothing is known) they move into the air like a cloud of golden brown, and when, in the evening, they settle down, the field or the tree they choose is transformed into this same golden brown. W. J. Holland reported having seen 'stunted trees on the New Jersey coast in the middle of October, when the foliage has already fallen, so completely covered with clinging masses of these butterflies as to present the appearance of trees in full leaf'.

29

With their strong wings beating in a steady rhythm, they can fly at a speed of twenty-five miles an hour, more than four times as fast as the ordinary cabbage butterfly. Upon reaching California or Florida, they seek out special trees where they settle so thickly that these trees have been called 'butterfly trees'. One place to which they have been travelling regularly for many years is the 'Butterfly Park' near the tip of the sunny Monterey Peninsula in California. One is reminded of the traditional coming of swallows to the Mission San Juan Capistrano in the same state.

The first documentary evidence of the Monarchs' coming to this place, called Pacific Grove, is dated 1881. Throughout the years they have always sought out the same grove of pine trees that their ancestors found before them. They arrive in mid-winter — when butterflies are seen hardly anywhere in the temperate zone — quite mysteriously, covering the neighbourhood with their golden wings, and they leave in the spring as mysteriously as they came. A local ordinance forbids, under a stiff penalty, any sort of disturbance of these visitors.

It is commonly assumed that most of the Monarchs which move south are the children and grandchildren of those that moved north in the spring; in the spring they fly north again and thus perform the amazing feat of a journey that may easily extend to over two thousand miles though many die by the way. We are far from knowing the exact flight or route of these tough little travellers, which traverse distances as great as from Hudson Bay to the Gulf of Mexico. Who guides them on their fantastic journeys, and who brings them with uncanny accuracy each year to the same trees? Nearly all the Monarchs, it must be re-emphasized, make the journey for the first time, and only once.

There is, apparently, no answer to this — no man has come close to solving this mystery, or that of the periodic movement of birds. However much entomologists have unearthed, these are secrets nature will not part with lightly.

There is no region on earth that can offer a richer variety of Lepidoptera than the tropics. This zone — a broad belt girdling the earth's surface extending twenty-three and a half degrees (about fifteen hundred miles) on each side of the Equator between the Tropic of Cancer on the north and of Capricorn on the south — includes part of Mexico, all of Central America, the larger part of South America, most of Africa, parts of Arabia, India, China, the entire Malay Archipelago, some of Australia, and many of the islands in the Pacific Ocean.

Travellers have expressed great excitement over one characteristic phenomenon of this zone: the almost impenetrable tangled wildernesses to which the Anglo-Indian term 'jungle' has been applied. Darwin was one of these admirers:

'Delight is a weak term to express the feelings of a naturalist who, for the first time, has wandered by himself in a Brazilian forest. The elegance of the grasses, the novelty of the parasitical plants, the beauty of the flowers, the glossy green of the foliage, but, above all, the general luxuriance of the vegetation, filled me with admiration.'

These tropical forests, steaming with moisture, are the habitat not only of towering palm trees, of panthers and tigers and birds of spectacular plumage, like the brilliant chromatic parrots and birds of paradise, but also of some of the most resplendent and most startling Lepidoptera. Alfred Russel Wallace noted how mousy and drab the butterflies of the temperate zone are when compared to their brethren in the torrid countries: 'Instead of the sober browns, the plain yellows, and the occasional patches of red or blue or orange that adorn our European species, we meet with the most intense metallic blues, the purest satiny greens, the most gorgeous crimsons . . .'

Of major importance to the history of the flying gems of the tropics are the names of Wallace, the 'high priest of entomology', and his colleague, Henry Walter Bates. Both were born in England, in 1823 and 1825 respectively, and both were in their early twenties when they met and determined to explore the wilderness of South America. Having little money, they expected to finance their expedition by the sale of duplicate specimens they hoped to capture. After spending two years together in the Amazon basin, they went different ways: Wallace took the Rio Negro and the upper waters of the Orinoco, while Bates continued his route up the great river Amazon for fourteen hundred miles.

Bates remained in Brazil for eleven years, during which time he collected no fewer than eight thousand species of insects new to science. With his health impaired, and in straitened circumstances, he returned to England, where he was fortunate enough to receive a post with the Royal Geographical Society, holding it until his death in 1892. At the prompting of his admirer, Darwin, he wrote *The Naturalist on the River Amazon* (1863). Two years earlier, he read before the Linnean Society a paper, 'Insect Fauna of the Amazon Valley', propounding the theory which became known as 'Batesian Mimicry'.

Wallace's experiences in South America can be learned from his *Travels on the Amazon and Rio Negro* (1853) and other books and articles. His extensive journeys through the East Indies were reported in *The Malay Archipelago* (1869). Wallace, who died in 1913 at the age of ninety, made many contributions to the natural sciences, especially to the theories of evolution, working out independently, but contemporaneously with Darwin, the theory of natural selection.

More than a hundred years have passed since the first pioneering exploits of Bates and Wallace and by now the museums of nearly every large city hold representative collections of tropical butterflies and moths. Now even youngsters are familiar with those flying jewels first captured by white men in the last century. Nothing can match the joyous discovery and direct observation of myriads of those remarkable creatures in their native forests, their pigmental colours unfaded and the structural hues scintillating like opals through the action of shafts of burning sunlight.

Bates found the environs of Pará (or Belém) in Brazil teeming with insect life. Pará, trading centre for the great region drained by the Amazon River, has more than three hundred thousand inhabitants. But when Bates visited it in the middle of the last century the town had a population of only twenty thousand and was still surrounded by dense woods:

'It will convey some idea of the diversity of butterflies when I mention that about seven hundred species of that tribe are found within an hour's walk of the town. . . . Some of the most showy species, such as the swallow-tailed kinds . . . are seen flying about the streets and gardens; sometimes they come through the open windows, attracted by flowers in the apartment. . . . It is in the height of the dry season that the greatest number and variety of butterflies are found in the woods; especially when a shower falls at intervals of a

32

THYSONOTIS APOLLONIUS FLDR.
Lycaenidae Blues
Distribution: *New Guinea, Aru Islands*

PAPILIO BIANOR CR.
Papilionidae Swallowtails
Distribution: *East Asia*
Caterpillar feeds on Aurantiaceen, Phellodendron

PSEUDACRAEA DOLOMENA HEW
Nymphalidae
Distribution: *Sierra Leone to Angola*

EUPHAEDRA MEDON L.
Nymphalidae
Distribution: *Sierra Leone to Angola*

few days. An infinite number of curious and rare species may then be taken, most diversified in habits, mode of flight, colours and markings; some yellow, others bright red, green, purple, and blue, and many bordered or spangled with metallic lines and spots of a silvery or golden lustre. Some have wings transparent as glass.'

He was even more enthusiastic after moving further inland:

'I found about five hundred and fifty distinct species of butterflies at Ega...eighteen species of the *Papilio* (the swallow-tail genus) can be found within ten minutes' walk of my house. No fact can speak more plainly for the surpassing exuberance of the vegetation, the varied nature of the land, the perennial warmth and humidity of the climate. But no description can convey an adequate notion of the beauty, and diversity in form and colour of this class of insects in the neighborhood of Ega.'

What a pity that none of the great poets of the Western world ever visited places like these. Bates himself was no poet, but occasionally the emotional impact of what he saw was so strong that he became lyrical, as, for instance, in this description of *Hetaera esmeralda* and its Protective Resemblance:

'It has one spot only of opaque colouring on its wings, which is of a violet and rose hue: this is the only part visible when the insect is flying low over dead leaves, in the gloomy shades where alone it is found, and it then looks like a wandering petal of a flower.'

The explorer, Everard Ferdinand im Thurn, was more interested in the aborigines than in the fauna of South America, yet he could not avoid noticing and being impressed by the 'huge *Morphos*, the large wings of which are entirely blue and so gorgeous, brilliant, and shining that the insect as it comes flaunting lazily down through the dark alleys between the tree-trunks, seems even from a considerable distance like a flash of blue light'. (From *Among the Indians of Guiana*, 1883.)

Some of the lovely Morphos of South America have since become rare through depredations of greedy hunters who gathered them for use as ornaments. The brilliantly coloured wings, or fragments of them, were mounted under glass to make brooches, pendants and trays. In fact, the danger of complete extinction was so serious that some South American governments passed laws prohibiting the capture and export of these species. Civilization is not an unmixed blessing; only a few decades ago, these Morphos existed in such multitudes in the valleys of the Amazon, the Orinoco and their tributaries that the step of an intruder would stir up swarms resembling floating flowers. In some of the forests they were so numerous that they formed the dominant feature of the landscape, compensating by their showy colours for the relative scarcity of flowers.

The inroads of civilization have, undoubtedly, decimated the lovely Lepidoptera in the eastern tropics as well. Among them are the Papilionidae, or Swallowtails, so called because their hinder wings are prolonged into 'tails'. They are also named 'bird-wing butterflies' for obvious reasons — their wings measure almost a foot from tip to tip. Wallace, who has given us more information about them than any other man, did not find them easy to capture. He wrote with curious candour of one experience:

'The beauty and brilliance of this insect are indescribable, and none but a naturalist can understand the intense excitement I experienced when I at length captured it. On taking it out of my net and opening the glorious wings, my heart began to beat violently, the blood rushed to my head, and I felt much more like fainting than I have done when in apprehension of immediate death. I had a headache the rest of the day, so great was the excitement produced by what will appear to most people a very inadequate cause.'

One of the butterflies he studied was Kallima, the dead-leaf butterfly mentioned in the section on Mimicry. Another he named after the Rajah of Sarawak, Sir James Brooke, an outstanding British soldier who spent most of his life fighting the wild tribes of Borneo. Today, however, *Papilio brookiana* is commonly known as 'Wallace's butterfly'. It is a real beauty, with velvety black and green wings and a black body with a crimson band around the neck like a cravat. It is also a curiosity, for, contrary to the general laws of nature, it is the female of this species that seeks and pursues the male. While this species lives predominantly in the jungle, it occasionally visits villages in search of garbage and dung.

Beautiful insects are also found in India. *Papilio blumei,* with its swallow-tail, and metallic green and blue patterns, ranks among the most delightful butterflies of the world. Another is *Teinopalpus imperialis* which, because of its extremely fast flight, is difficult to capture. Indian, too, is that gigantic moth, *Attacus atlas.* The world's most glamorous moth, *Argema mittrei,* however, is to be found off the east coast of Africa, on the island of Madagascar.

Many of the tropical Lepidoptera have interesting living habits, especially that of 'aestivating' (the reverse of hibernating). In summer they seek spots sheltered from the scorching heat of the sun and remain quiescent until, with the advent of the rainy season, the vegetation breaks once more into vigorous growth. The males of the Nymphalidae live in the crowns of the forest trees, while the females are hidden in the bushes. They descend to the ground only for mating, or for the moisture of pools or streams.

Mr Wallace would have loved a book like this, in which out of the hundred and thirty-seven butterflies and moths depicted and described half come from the regions he loved so much, South America and the Malay

ACRAEA ANACREON TRIM
Nymphalidae
Distribution: *South Africa up to the Transvaal, Malawi, and German East Africa*

PIECIS CERYNE BSD
Nymphalidae
Distribution: *Africa; along the Niger, Cameroon*

CHARAXES IASIUS L.
Nymphalidae
Distribution: *Greece, Italy, Southern France, Spain,*
North Africa up to Syria
Caterpillar feeds on Strawberry plants

DANAIS CHRYSIPPUS L.
Danaidae
Distribution: *Asia, Africa, China, Japan, Australia,*
(Europe: Italy)
Caterpillar feeds on Asclepiadaceen (dog's-bane)

Archipelago. He remained struck by the beauty he had seen in his younger years, and he was in his late eighties when he wrote:

'Nature has . . . used them [the butterflies], like the pages of illuminated missals, to exhibit all her powers in the production, on a miniature scale, of the utmost possibilities of colour decoration, colour variety, and of colour beauty, and has done this by a method which appears to us to be unnecessarily complex and supremely difficult, in order perhaps to lead us to recognize some guiding power, some Supreme Mind, directing and organizing the blind forces of nature in the production of this marvellous development of life and loveliness.'

IN POETRY, ART AND LORE

When we think of the part the butterfly has played in the arts of the Western world, we are reminded of Puccini's opera, which is still as lovely and as enchanting as it was when it was first performed more than a half century ago. But it has nothing to do with butterflies except for the nickname, 'Madame Butterfly', given to the gay and affectionate Japanese heroine, Cho-Cho-San, who is fated at the end to kill herself with her father's sword. Yet for a long time, poets have been fascinated by the Lepidopteron's metamorphoses, and held spellbound by the glowing colours and intricate designs of a Lepidopteron's wing. This is especially true of the sophisticated ancient civilizations of the Far East, in China and Indo-China, in Korea and Japan, where butterflies and moths can be found that are more attractive than those of Europe. In a few lines, a Japanese poet likens the glittering butterfly to a silken shawl gliding off the shoulders of a beautiful woman. Many similar poems are short, concise and so tender that they can no more be translated into another language than the scales from a butterfly's wing can be transferred to a brush in order to paint with them. In the Western world, it was not until the Renaissance and the discovery of nature that poets gave the butterfly its due praise. There are no attractive moths to be found in the Mediterranean world or in the Northern parts of Europe, and wherever the moth is mentioned in poetry, it is only as a pest. All poets echo the sentiments of the prophet Isaiah, who thus refers to the enemies of Israel: 'They all shall wax old as a garment; the moth shall eat them up.' The Bible makes not a single mention of the butterfly, and puritan society, based on the Holy Scriptures, laying stress on industry and condemning laziness, naturally preferred the ant, which builds colonies and gathers and stores food, or the bee, which produces honey and wax. The great English poets — among them Shakespeare, Spenser, Wordsworth, Shelley and Keats — celebrated the beauty of butterflies, although they were acquainted with only the relatively drab species of so northern a country as England.

There are also many charming references to butterflies in American prose and poetry. Perhaps the most striking of these is that of Walt Whitman. In his *Specimen Days,* he wrote:

'Over all flutter myriads of light-yellow butterflies, mostly skimming along the surface, dipping and

40

oscillating, giving a curious animation to the scene. The beautiful, spiritual insects! straw-color'd Psyches! Occasionally one of them leaves his mates, and mounts, perhaps spirally, perhaps in a straight line in the air, fluttering up, up, till literally out of sight. In the lane as I came along just now I noticed one spot, ten feet square or so, where more than a hundred had collected, holding a revel, a gyration-dance, or butterfly good-time, winding and circling, down and across, but always keeping within the limits.'
'Butterflies and butterflies . . . continue to flit to and fro, all sorts, white, yellow, brown, purple—now and then some gorgeous fellow flashing lazily by on wings like artists' palettes dabb'd with every color.'

The beauty and grace of Lepidoptera have induced artists of all nations in all ages to try to capture their essence in painting and sculpture. They have also influenced folk art. Since the butterfly plays a considerable role in the American Indian's customs and lore of today, archaeologists were not surprised to find on the sites of ancient Indian villages and in burial places prehistoric ceremonial objects resembling butterflies with spread wings ('Butterfly stones'). The butterfly and moth motif can be noted on painted pottery, basketry, bead work, and woven fabrics made by the Indians of today. Blackfoot Indians often carve the butterfly symbol—an eight-pointed design somewhat resembling the Maltese Cross—below the smoke vent at the back of their lodges. Mothers of this tribe embroider the sign of the butterfly in beads or quills on a small piece of buckskin, and tie this in the baby's hair in order to make him sleep (the butterfly is believed to bring dreams).

Often it was the religious symbolism assigned to the butterfly that required artists to pay attention to it. In ancient Greece, Psyche, the personification of the human soul, was frequently presented in art as a maiden with butterfly wings, or simply as a butterfly. On an ancient cameo Eros is shown trying to catch a butterfly, a reference to the Eros and Psyche legend. On sarcophagi can be found carvings which represent the soul as a butterfly hovering over a corpse, a skeleton or a skull. Today, entomologists call a large family of hairy moths, popularly known as bagmoths or bagworms, Psychidae.

According to the concept of Christian theology, man, like the butterfly, must pass through two preparatory stages; life, symbolized by the caterpillar, and death, by the chrysalis, before the soul reaches its goal—resurrection, symbolized in Christian iconography by the perfected imago. On a gravestone in an old cemetery in Basle can be seen the sculptured representation of this concept: above the shrouded chrysalis is the soaring butterfly. Paintings of the Virgin and the Child often show a butterfly held in the hand of the Child, a symbol of the Resurrection of Christ.

In the Renaissance, however, artists often included beautiful butterflies in their paintings without necessarily attaching to them a special symbolic meaning, just as they filled spaces with other animals or with flowers and fruit. Insects of all sorts were also depicted, with great care, in illuminated manuscripts. The Dutch, who were (as they still are) passionate gardeners, included butterflies in many of the flowerpieces painted in seventeenth- and eighteenth-century Holland. Painters from Brueghel to Jan van Huysum loved to paint bouquets of many flowers in fine vases, set on marble tables and adorned with butterflies sipping nectar from blossoms or soaring above them, drawn with such extraordinary realism that one could almost reach for a net.

Butterflies appear in the delicate flowerpieces of that great mystic among moderns, the Frenchman Odilon Redon, and in many of the oils and watercolours of his compatriot, Raoul Dufy.

Whistler's famous butterfly signature was developed out of a kind of Eastern design containing his initials and drawn for him by his friend, the pre-Raphaelite Rossetti.

'The drawing appealed to Whistler, who developed the idea until, out of the letters J. M. W., something like a butterfly appeared. The insect became more and more clearly defined, and gradually he perfected it to his own satisfaction. In time it appeared as an important detail in all his pictures, and eventually it adorned his books and took the place of his ordinary signature in his letters to the press and his private correspondence.' Hesketh Pearson, who wrote this, added that the advent of the butterfly was not a coincidence, but corresponded with the artist's mood: 'He too showed a desire to flit without apparent purpose.'

In the Far East, the butterfly often appears on porcelain of the Ch'ing dynasty (1644 — 1911), especially since the butterfly was considered a symbol of longevity — its name has the same sound as the word meaning 'sixty years of age'. Elegant pictures of the butterfly appear in Chinese and Japanese brush drawings and also in woodcuts, and on kakemonos, those long silken scrolls that are hung on walls.

The fascinating life and development of the butterfly provided the sages of India and China with food for thought. The mythology of Hinduism relates that Brahma, while dwelling on earth, watched the greedy caterpillars in his vegetable garden and saw them turn into pupae and finally butterflies. Seeing this, his heart was filled with great calm, and henceforth he looked forward to his own perfection in his final

PAPILIO ANTHEUS CR.
Papilionidae Swallowtails
Distribution: *Sierra Leone to Angola*
Caterpillar feeds on Artabotrys (Anonaceen)

PAPILIO SARPEDON L.
Papilionidae Swallowtails
Distribution: *Hainan, Tonkin, Northern India to the Philippines and Lombok*

CYSTINEURA DORCAS F.
Nymphalidae
Distribution: *Jamaica*

PAPILIO AEGEUS DON
Papilionidae Swallowtails
Distribution: *Queensland, New South Wales*

incarnation. Likewise, Chuang Tzu, the most original of Taoist philosophers, who loved to take his similes from the world of nature around him, uses the butterfly for his allegories. He was himself nicknamed the 'Butterfly Philosopher', for he once dreamed that he had been transformed into a butterfly and had found great happiness in flitting hither and thither, sipping nectar from innumerable flowers.

Among the Mexicans, both the earth-mothers and the fire-gods have butterflies for their insignia. A tribe on the Indonesian island of Sumatra relates that the world's first three men were born from three eggs laid by a giant butterfly.

From religion and philosophy it is only a very short step to folklore, and the superstitions of all nations have references to butterflies. In Westphalia in Germany, the butterfly is a symbol of evil, and on St Peter's Day (22nd of February) children go from house to house, knocking on the doors with hammers and singing comic rhymes in which they bid the *suentevoegel* (also called *sunnenvoegel* or *sommervoegel)* to depart. Or the inhabitants themselves go all through the house, knocking on all the doors, to drive away these 'birds'. If this ceremony is omitted, misfortune may be the consequence.

As a rule, however, the butterfly is a symbol of the soul of the departed ones. According to Finno-Ugric mythology, the soul departs from a dead body in the shape of a butterfly; but even the soul of a sleeping man can issue from his mouth, drink water from a well or pond, and return to the sleeper. In the Solomon Islands, in the South Pacific, a dying man would tell the members of his family in which shape he intended to transmigrate — it might be as a bird, or a butterfly. Henceforth, the family would consider this particular species sacred and refrain from injuring it.

The Slavs open a door or a window to permit the soul, often in the shape of a butterfly, to leave the body of a dead man. In Hawaii we find a version of the Orpheus and Eurydice myth in the tale of Hiku and his wife, Kawelu. After Kawelu's death, Hiku went down to the underworld where he caught the soul of his beloved transformed into a butterfly. He returned to the corpse, made a hole in the great toe of the left foot, forced the spirit to enter, and thus brought her back to life.

There are butterfly dances among the Japanese, and among the Indians of northwestern Brazil. The Japanese dance was derived from India, Indo-China, China and Korea: colour prints show human beings with butterfly wings whirling among flowers. In a Brazilian dance supposed to honour the dead, the masked dancers will imitate the actions and habits of birds, beasts and insects:

'For example, there is a large azure-blue butterfly which delights the eye with the splendour of its colour,

45

like a fallen fragment of the sky; and in the butterfly dance two men represent the play of these brilliant insects in the sunshine, fluttering on the wing and settling on sandbanks and rocks.' (From Fraser's *The Golden Bough.*)

There exists a Butterfly clan of the Hopi Indians which regards the butterfly as a totem. Every year, these Indians carry out a butterfly dance on the open plaza of their village. This dance, supposed to bring good crops, is performed throughout an entire day by young men and girls, while the older generation watch from the rooftops of the houses.

Countless other superstitions connected with butterflies and moths are observed among civilized nations and the so-called savages alike. In Oldenburg in Germany, the first butterfly of the season should be caught and made to fly through the coat sleeve. In Iglau in Moravia, a hunter will put a butterfly into the barrel of his gun to ensure his aim. In Essex, people are advised, for good luck, to catch the first white butterfly, to bite off its head, and let it go. In one place, a butterfly means good luck, in another it is regarded as a bad omen. It is credited variously with bringing babies, foretelling death, promising fair or predicting wet weather. Among the dark men in the Congo area and in the Cameroons, the large *Drurya antimachus* is feared as the God of Revenge; in Madagascar a certain large moth is shunned as the messenger of bad luck and death. Among the Slavs the Noctuidae, large moths that are reminiscent of owls (hence the name) are believed to be incubi molesting and disturbing the sleeper. *Acherontia atropos,* whose back is marked with a death's head, is reputed to bring death.

It is interesting how different creeds interpret the migrations of butterflies. In Ceylon, the Buddhists believe that the butterflies proceed to the top of a mountain called Adam's Peak where they do homage to the 'footstep of Buddha,' to return purged of their sins. Among the Malays, who are Mohammedans, the idea persists that the butterflies' flight amounts to a yearly pilgrimage to Mecca.

But these are only a few, a very few samples of the role played by the Lepidoptera in man's metaphysical world, as expressed in fables and tales, poetry and prose, music and art.

46

PRECIS CLELIA CR.
Nymphalidae
Distribution: *Africa, Comoro Islands, Socotra, Aldabra*

PAPILIO DEMOLEUS L.
Papilionidae Swallowtails
Distribution: *China, Southern India, Ceylon, Persia, Muscat*
Caterpillar feeds on Citrus, Glyrosmis, Myrrayia, Ruta angushfolia

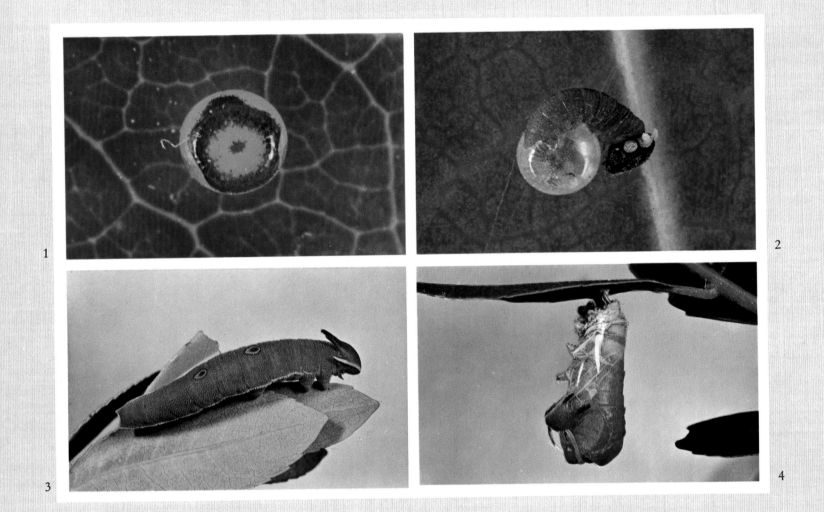

1 2
3 4

Developmental stages
of a Butterfly

CHAIAXES IASIUS L.
Nymphalidae
Distribution: *Greece, Italy, Southern France, Spain,*
North Africa and Middle East north to Syria
Caterpillar feeds on strawberry plants

5

6

7

8

Plate 1 Egg
Plate 2 Caterpillar hatching
Plate 3 Caterpillar
Plate 4 Caterpillar turning into a chrysalis

Plate 5 Butterfly hatching
Plate 6 Butterfly hatched out
Plate 7 Butterfly, seen from below
Plate 8 Butterfly top view

JOSEF BIJOK · DEVELOPMENTAL STAGES OF BUTTERFLIES

Butterflies and moths belong to one of the largest of the many classes of the animal kingdom, the Insects. In geological time the first vague traces of them occur in the Cretaceous period, but it was not until the Tertiary epoch that they really appeared as a well developed order evolving parallel with the flowering plants which they helped to pollinate.

THE BODY of a butterfly is made up of three parts all of which are clothed in scales, or scales modified in the form of hair. The freely movable head bears the compound (faceted) eyes, the feelers, and the mouth parts consisting of palpi and proboscis. The thorax (chest) is solidly formed of three segments fused together each of which bears a pair of legs and two of which (the middle and last) also each bear a pair of wings. The abdomen (body) contains the digestive and reproductive organs. The four wings, like the body, are also covered with scales, and from this fact is derived the scientific name of the order Lepidoptera (Greek *lepis,* a scale; *pteron,* a wing), which embraces both the butterflies and the moths. From the developmental point of view a butterfly during its life passes through four distinct and sharply separated stages, egg (ovum), caterpillar (larva), chrysalis (pupa) and perfect insect (imago). In other words, butterflies undergo complete metamorphosis.

THE ANTENNAE are made up of many segments all of which may bear sense organs in the form of tactile hairs or bristles, olfactory pits and cones. They exhibit great variety of form, often differing widely even in the two sexes of a single species, and for this reason are of great use in classification. In form they may be clavate (club-shaped), capitate (knobbed), filiform (thread-like), setaceous (bristly), fusiform (spindle-shaped), serrated (saw-like), pectinate (comb-like), dentate (toothed), plumose (feathered), or bipectinate (double-combed), to mention only the principal variations. The coiled proboscis, or tongue, lies coiled like a spring between the palpi, the shape of which is also important in classification.

THE LEGS of many species bear stout spines, and the last segments forming the tarsus are frequently provided with sense organs, especially of taste. The tarsi of the forelegs are often much modified and in the so-called 'brush-footed' Nymphalid butterflies the male tarsus is reduced to a brush and the female's ends in a comb-like formation.

THE WINGS of the Lepidoptera develop from minute infoldings of the skin which are first formed during the caterpillar stage. Through the wings, between their upper and lower surfaces, there runs a network of veins. The pattern formed by this network displays such regularity that it provides most valuable classificatory characters. The wing-scales which are arranged in an orderly fashion like the tiles on the roof of a house, are formed by minute outgrowths from the underlying surfaces. Some of the colours are produced by pigments contained within the scales, sometimes by a combination of several pigments.

The dazzling 'metallic' blue, violet, silver and gold colours on the other hand are 'interference colours', i.e. the light waves are broken up by the minute structure of the scales, as by the surface of a soap-bubble. Sometimes the colour is produced by the combination of a pigment and an interference effect. Often the wings, like other parts of the body, carry scent organs, either in the form of scent scales or, more elaborately, scent glands associated with a pencil of hairs which opens to disseminate the scent. Such scents are believed to be used in courtship displays and to attract the other sex.

THE EGG After mating, the female butterfly lays her eggs on the leaves, flowers or stems of the plant on which the caterpillar will feed after hatching. They may be laid singly, in groups or neat rows, sometimes as bracelets around a twig, sometimes on the bark of trees or even on stones. Some moths even scatter their eggs broadcast when in flight, but most are securely cemented to the surface on which they are laid. In some cases they are covered with hairs from the female's abdomen to serve as a protection against enemies, inclement weather or the rigours of winter.

Eggs take many shapes, though constant for each species. They may be spherical, hemispherical, disc-, barrel- or pear-shaped, elipsoid or conical, but always at the upper end minute pores can be seen through which the male sperm enters to fertilise the egg before it is laid. Infertile eggs never hatch and often collapse soon after being laid. Fertile eggs maintain their shape, and usually change colour slowly as the caterpillar developing inside begins to take shape and colour.

THE CATERPILLAR On hatching from the egg the young caterpillar frequently eats the remains of its egg-shell as its first meal. It should have no distance to go in search of its next meal since its egg was probably laid on its foodplant. The general shape of a caterpillar needs no description, but when resting it often adopts an attitude quite different from that when actively moving. Its most important mouth-parts are, naturally, its jaws (mandibles), since its only function in life is to eat. Flanking these are a pair of tiny palpi, and above and below these the upper (labrum) and lower (labium) lips. Associated with the latter is the spinneret through which the familiar silken thread of caterpillars is spun. The first three pairs of legs differ from all the others and are known as true legs: they correspond to the butterfly's legs. The other legs are usually called the abdominal legs, or prolegs, and do not re-appear in the butterfly. These usually number ten, arranged in a group of four pairs with a fifth pair at the anal extremity. In the larvae of Geometrid moths the first three pairs of prolegs are missing, so that they move with the peculiar gait that has earned them both the popular name of 'loopers', and their scientific name, Geometer, i.e. earth-measurer. Very few caterpillars are entirely naked; most of them are covered with hair, bristles or spines, the latter often branched, pencil-like tufts of hair, fleshy tubercles or warts. Most Hawk moth caterpillars have a characteristic horn at the anal end of the body, and when at rest adopt the sphinx-like attitude which has given them their scientific name, Sphingidae. The caterpillar of the Puss Moth can spray an attacker with 30–40% formic acid and shoot out from its forked tail a pair of bright red filaments.

Not all caterpillars feed exclusively on plants. Some at times, others habitually, eat other insects or even other caterpillars. Some bore in wood or feed on products which man stores for his own use, or on the wax in bee-hives etc. Many caterpillars are monophagous, that is to say they will only eat one particular kind of plant, and will die of starvation rather than eat another. Most species, however, are polyphagous and can live on a wide variety of plants. Many caterpillars make silken webs on which to rest, especially when moulting, others make a common web within which they live. Some, which spend the winter as caterpillars, make silken nests called hibernacula. Silken threads are also used as a means of escape from danger. During growth caterpillars moult four or five times. Just before doing so they cease to feed for a while then, at the right moment, the skin behind the head splits and by degrees the caterpillar creeps out of the old skin leaving it behind, complete in every detail and still firmly attached to its silken carpet. The new skin quickly hardens, and may be quite different from the old one in colour and ornamentation.

THE PUPA Shortly before turning into a chrysalis caterpillars cease feeding and become restless in search of a suitable place for pupation. The larvae of most butterflies pupate above ground, attached to a stem or leaf of their foodplant. Those of the Swallowtails spin a silken girdle round the waist which holds them upright against a stalk. Those of the Nymphalidae, such as the Camberwell Beauty, Peacock, Large and Small Tortoiseshells fasten their hindlegs firmly to a support from which they hang upside down, like a sausage in a butcher's shop. They remain like this for a day or two whilst the breakdown of tissues which leads to the formation of the butterfly begins internally. Eventually the skin splits along the back and with many shakings and wrigglings the old skin is gradually cast off disclosing an angular limbless chrysalis which is often ornamented with flecks and projections of shining gold and silver.

Caterpillars of the Hawk moths and the night-flying Noctuidae burrow into the soil and fashion for themselves more or less roomy chambers in which to pupate. Others spin a light cocoon amongst moss and withered leaves on the surface of the soil. The caterpillars of the Bombyces – a term which includes a number of families of stout-bodied moths – have strongly developed silk glands that enable them to spin stout cocoons which are sometimes very tough. The Silk Moth itself belongs to this group as well as several other species the silk of which is sometimes used commercially.

The pupal stage may vary from as little as two or three weeks to as much as several years, depending on the species. It is the stage in which most moths pass the winter, although many do so as larvae. Some Tiger Moths even over-winter two or three times as larvae. The frosts of winter are a direct necessity for some species; they cannot survive unless subjected to them. Slowly the butterfly within the pupal skin begins to take shape until shortly before emergence the colours of the wings begin to show through the wing sheaths. At last, the pupal skin splits at the thorax, the antennae appear and the first legs reach out to seek a foothold. Slowly, with an obvious effort, the butterfly frees itself and climbs out, the tiny bag-like wings hanging from the thorax. Having obtained a firm foothold, the butterfly begins to expand its wings by pumping its body fluid through them. In a few minutes they begin to take shape, but it is some hours before they harden enough for the butterfly to stretch them and trust to them in flight. Before flying away, waste products of the process of metamorphosis have to be evacuated through the anus. This substance, known as the meconium, is usually pink or reddish, and in olden times gave rise to the

52

belief in 'red rain'. Having completed all these processes the butterfly, now sexually mature, can fly off in search of nectar or honey and a mate. Hawk moths, however, must first 'warm up' by vigorously vibrating their wings. The rate of wing beat per second may vary from 7 to 8 in a White or Clouded Yellow Butterfly to 70 or 80 in the Humming Bird Hawk Moth. The buzzing noise made by a large Hawk Moth in flight is very clearly audible.

Once the male has found his bride, attracted by her use of her scent organs, and mating has taken place, the whole life cycle starts all over again.

THE PRINCIPAL FAMILIES OF BUTTERFLIES AND LARGE MOTHS (LEPIDOPTERA)

BUTTERFLIES (Rhopalocera)		
	Papilionidae	Swallowtails
	Pieridae	Whites
	Danaidae	Milkweeds
	Satyridae	Browns and Ringlets
	Morphidae	Morphos
	Nymphalidae	Nymphalids
	Lycaenidae	Blues
	Hesperiidae	Skippers

MOTHS (Heterocera)		
	Sphingidae	Hawk Moths
	Notodontidae	Prominents
	Lymantriidae	Tussocks
	Lasiocampidae	Lappets
	Saturniidae	Emperor Moths
	Drepanidae	Hooktips
	Noctuidae	Noctuids
	Geometridae	Geometers (Carpets)
	Arctiidae	Tiger Moths
	Zygaenidae	Burnets
	Psychidae	Bagworms
	Sesiidae	Clearwings
	Cossidae	Goat Moths
	Hepialidae	Swifts

PLATES OF BUTTERFLIES AND MOTHS

Plate 1

EUROPEAN BUTTERFLIES

ORANGE TIP
Anthocharis cardamines (Pieridae)
Foodplants, various Crucifers e.g.
Lady's Smock, Hedge Mustard,
Wild Charlock.
Pupa held upright to stem of food
plant by silken girdle.
Flies in May and June.
The female lacks the orange patch
on the forewing.

LARGE WHITE
Pieris brassicae (Pieridae)
The caterpillar is a pest of
cabbages.
The butterfly flies in May and in a
second generation in August.
It is a migrant.

LARGE TORTOISESHELL
*Nymphalis polychloros
(Nymphalidae)*
Caterpillars on elm, cherry and
other trees in a loose web.
Butterfly in July and again in
spring after hibernation.

SMALL TORTOISESHELL
Aglais urticae (Nymphalidae)
The spiney caterpillars are
gregarious and feed on
Stinging Nettles.
There are two, sometimes three
generations each year.
Flies in spring, midsummer and
autumn.

SCARCE SWALLOWTAIL
Papilio podalirius (Papilionidae)
Common in central and
southern Europe. Flies in
spring an again in late summer.
Caterpillar feeds on foliage of
plum, apple, pear and oak trees.

THE SWALLOWTAIL
Papilio machaon (Papilionidae)
The green, black-banded
caterpillar feeds on wild carrot.
Though widespread abroad,
in England confined to Norfolk.
Usually flies in two generations,
spring and late summer.

THAIS POLYXENA
Thais polyxena (Papilionidae)
Flies in June and July in southern
Europe from S. France eastwards.
Caterpillar on Birthwort
(*Aristolochia clematitis*).

PARNASSIUS APOLLO
Parnassius apollo (Papilionidae)
An alpine butterfly.
Eggs laid on White Stonecrop hatch
the following spring.
Pupa in a loose cocoon on the
ground.
Flies in July and August.

CLOUDED YELLOW
Colias crocea (Pieridae)
Formerly known as *Colias edusa*.
Migrates northward from
S. Europe every year.
Two generations, June and August.
Caterpillar on lucerne and clovers.

BRIMSTONE
Gonepteryx rhamni (Pieridae)
Flies in June and July and again in
the spring after hibernation.
Caterpillar feeds on buckthorn.
Female paler yellow than the male.

BLACK-VEINED WHITE
Aporia crataegi (Pieridae)
Caterpillar is gregarious and often
a pest of orchard trees.
Extinct in British Isles.
Flies in June and July.

PEACOCK
Vanessa io (Nymphalidae)
Spiney caterpillar feeds
gregariously on stinging nettle.
Butterfly emerges in late summer
and reappears in spring after
hibernation.

COMMA
Polygonia c-album (Nymphalidae)
The spiney caterpillar has a broad
white patch on the back and feeds
on elm, hop and nettle.
The generations of the Comma are
complicated, but essentially consist
of one in early summer and a
second which hibernates and
reappears in spring.

Plate 2

EUROPEAN BUTTERFLIES

HEATH FRITILLARY
Melitaea athalia (Nymphalidae)
Abroad a common butterfly with
spring and summer generations.
In England rare and very local
with a single generation
in June and July.
Foodplants plantains, cow-wheat.

PURPLE EMPEROR
Apatura iris (Nymphalidae)
Caterpillar feeds on sallow and
hibernates when very small.
Butterfly frequents old woodlands
in July and August, feeding on
decomposing animal droppings etc.
Female lacks the blue flush
of the male.

PARARGE HIERA
Pararge hiera (Satyridae)
Closely related to the Wall Brown
which occurs in Britain.
Rather a mountain butterfly, with
two broods, May to June and
August–September.
Foodplant, fescue grass.

PAINTED LADY
Vanessa cardui (Nymphalidae)
A great migrant, reaching Britain
in most years, almost cosmopolitan.
Number of broods varies from
place to place.
Fails to hibernate in northern
countries.
Larva feeds on thistles.

CAMBERWELL BEAUTY
Nymphalis antiopa (Nymphalidae)
A rare migrant in Britain.
Widespread abroad.
Flies from midsummer onwards
and again in spring after
hibernation.
Foodplant, sallow.

ARGYNNIS NIOBE
Argynnis niobe (Nymphalidae)
Woodland and mountain meadows
throughout Europe,
but not in Britain.
Very similar to the
British High Brown Fritillary.
Larva on violet.

MARBLED WHITE
Melanargia galathea (Satyridae)
A denizen of meadows and places
where the grasses abound which are
the larva's foodplant.
Hibernates as a caterpillar and
pupates on the surface of the soil.

LIMENITIS POPULI
Limenitis populi (Nymphalidae)
Flies in midsummer onwards in
most European countries, but not
in Britain, especially near water.
The caterpillar feeds on poplar.

GRAYLING
Satyrus semele (Satyridae)
A late summer butterfly with a
habit of resting on hot stony
ground with wings closed and
pointing to the sun so that it is very
difficult to see.
Larva on grasses.

SILVER-WASHED
FRITILLARY
Argynnis paphia (Nymphalidae)
Flies from late June to August.
The egg, often laid on the bark of
a tree hatches quickly, but the
young larva goes at once into
hibernation without feeding.
Foodplant, violets.

ADONIS BLUE
Lysandra bellargus (Lycaenidae)
The caterpillar feeds exclusively on
Horseshoe Vetch, and hibernates.
Butterfly is on the wing in
May–June and again in September.
Associated particularly with chalk
downland and limestone country.

RED ADMIRAL
Vanessa atalanta (Nymphalidae)
Two generations, but most
commonly seen in late summer and
autumn feeding on Michaelmas
Daisies or buddleia.
A migrant which rarely survives
the English winter.
Larva on stinging nettles.

LYCAENA VIRGAUREAE
Lycaena virgaureae (Lycaenidae)
A close relative of the extinct
British Large Copper.
Common on the continent of
Europe in flowery meadows up to
7–8,000 ft. in July and August.
Foodplant, sorrel.

WHITE ADMIRAL
Limenitis sibilla (Nymphalidae)
Caterpillar feeds on honeysuckle
and hibernates when quite small.
Butterfly has a gliding flight, flies
in midsummer, and is a denizen of
woodlands.

ARASCHNIA LEVANA
Araschnia levana (Nymphalidae)
The spring brood is illustrated.
The summer brood is black and
very different.
Feeds on stinging nettles.
Throughout Europe, except the
British Isles.

Plate 3

EUROPEAN MOTHS

POPLAR HAWK
Smerinthus populi (Sphingidae)
Larva on poplar.
Pupates in the ground.
Flies in May – July.

BUFF TIP
Phalera bucephala (Notodontidae)
When resting on ground in-
distinguishable from a broken twig.
Flies in May – July.
Caterpillars feed on foliage of
almost any tree.

LIME HAWK
Mimas tiliae (Sphingidae)
Flies principally in May and June.
Common.
Larva on lime, sometimes elm.

PTEROGON PROSERPINA
Pterogon proserpina (Sphingidae)
Not British, but common in most
central and southern European
countries.
Food plant: willow herb and
evening primrose.

BLACK ARCHES
*Lymantria monacha
(Lymantriidae)*
Flies in July and August.
Caterpillar in parts of Europe is a
pest of coniferous trees.

JASPIDEA CELSIA
Jaspidea celsia (Noctuidae)
An eastern and northern species,
just reaching Scandinavia,
E. Germany and the Alps.
Flies in August – September.
Food plant: grasses.

PRIVET HAWK
Sphinx ligustri (Sphingidae)
Flies in June and July.
Larva on privet, sometimes lilac.

DEATH'S HEAD
Acherontia atropos (Sphingidae)
The markings on the thorax give it
its name, and its quite false
reputation as a harbinger of evil.
A migrant which reaches England
from S. Europe most years.
Caterpillar feeds on potato haulm,
and buries itself deeply in the soil
to pupate.

OLEANDER HAWK
Daphnis nerii (Sphingidae)
A Mediterranean species which
only reaches England as a very rare
migrant.
Oleander is the food plant
of the larva.

EYED HAWK
Smerinthus ocellatus (Sphingidae)
Flies in May – July.
Foodplant: willow, sallow.

CONVOLVULUS HAWK
Herse convulvuli (Sphingidae)
Not native, but migrants from
southern Europe reach Britain
most years.
Two brooded, May – June,
August – September.
Larva on Convolvulus.

PINE HAWK
Hyloicus pinastri (Sphingidae)
Flies in May – July.
Much commoner in England
now than formerly.
Larva feeds on needles of
Scotch Fir and other pines.

ELEPHANT HAWK
Chaerocampa elpenor (Sphingidae)
Flies in May – June.
Rarely two-brooded.
Larva feeds on willow herb
principally.

SPURGE HAWK
Deilephila euphorbiae (Sphingidae)
Moth occurs from May till autumn.
Larva on Spurge.
Pupa may hibernate several years.
A very rare immigrant to
southern England.

HUMMING BIRD HAWK MOTH
*Macroglossa stellatarum
(Sphingidae)*
Its characteristic flight gives this
sun-loving hawkmoth its name.
Double-brooded:
June – July, August – September.
Larva on bedstraw.

MAGPIE
*Abraxas grossulariata
(Geometridae)*
A common distasteful to birds;
moth flies in June to August.
Larva on currant, gooseberry,
Euonymus, sloe, hawthorn etc.

PEACH BLOSSOM
Thyatira batis (Thyatiridae)
April – May.
Larva on bramble and raspberry.

Plate 4

EUROPEAN MOTHS

LARGE EMERALD
Geometra papilionaria
(Geometridae)
Flies in July and August
in woodlands.
Larva feeds on birch, alder, hazel
and beech, and pupates amongst
leaves.

THE EMPEROR MOTH
Female
Saturnia pavonia (Saturniidae)
In May and June the male flies by
day in search of the female.
Caterpillar feeds on bramble and
sloe and spins a very tough brown
cocoon.

AGLIA TAU
Aglia tau (Saturniidae)
Male flies by day in open
woodlands in March to June.
Larva feeds on oak,
beech and birch.

PERICALLIA MATRONULA
Pericallia matronula (Arctiidae)
Found chiefly in central European
highlands in June and July.
Sometimes flies by day.
Larva hibernates twice.

TIGER MOTH
Arctia caja (Arctiidae)
Flies from June to August.
The 'woolly bear' caterpillar feeds
on a wide variety of low-growing
plants.

SCARLET TIGER
Panaxia dominula (Arctiidae)
Flies in July.
Caterpillar hibernates and feeds on
bramble, stinging nettle, blackthorn
and various low-growing plants.

CATOCALA FULMINEA
Catocala fulminea (Noctuidae)
Flies in July and August.
Larva on sloe and plum.

KENTISH GLORY
Endromis versicolora (Endromidae)
Very local in Britain, in April, the
male flying by day.
Birch and alder.
Stout cocoon in surface litter.

ODEZIA TIBIALE
Odezia tibiale (Geometridae)
Flies in damp woodland glades
in June and July.
Larva on baneberry.

OAK EGGAR
Male
Lasiocampa quercus
(Lasiocampidae)
Flies in July and August in open
deciduous forest, the larva feeding
on oak, hawthorn and sloe.
Pupates in a hard brown oval
cocoon on the surface of the ground.

ESSEX EMERALD
Euchloris smaragdaria
(Geometridae)
In England only found in Essex
marshes, in July, where the larva
feeds on sea wormwood.

Plate 5

EUROPEAN MOTHS

LEMONIA DUMI
Lemonia dumi (Lemoniidae)
Flies only in October and
November.
Food plant: hawkweed.

DARK CRIMSON UNDERWING
Catocala sponsa (Noctuidae)
Flies in July and August.
In England only in New Forest.
Larva on oak and chestnut.

LARGE YELLOW UNDERWING
Triphaena pronuba (Noctuidae)
Flies from midsummer to late
autumn.
The larva feeds on most
low-growing plants.

SATURNIA PYRI
Saturnia pyri (Saturniidae)
The largest European moth.
Flies in spring and again (rarely)
in autumn.
Larva feeds on fruit trees.

JERSEY TIGER
*Callimorpha quadripunctaria
(Arctiidae)*
On the wing from June to
September.
Likes moist woodland gullies.
In England confined to S. Devon.
Larva feeds at night on
low-growing plants.

CREAM-SPOT TIGER
Arctia villica (Arctiidae)
Flies in June and July.
The larva, which hibernates, feeds
on most low-growing plants.

CLIFDEN NONPAREIL
Catocala fraxini (Noctuidae)
A rare immigrant which sometimes
breeds in southern England,
the larva feeding on aspen.

ARCTIA FLAVIA
Arctia flavia (Arctiidae)
Found in July and August in
Europe only in the Alps.
Food plant: dandelion.

OAK EGGAR
Female
*Lasiocampa quercus
(Lasiocampidae)*
Flies in July and August in open
deciduous forest, the larva feeding
on oak, hawthorn and sloe.
Pupa in hard brown cocoon on
surface of the ground.

Plate 6

ARMANDIA LIDDERDALEI, The Bhutan Glory

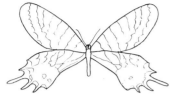

Distribution: *Bhutan, Naga Hills, mountainous regions in North-East Assam?, China, Burma.* Although it is not a true Swallowtail Butterfly this species belongs to the very large Papilionid family. The wings are of a very unusual and curious shape, the body is clad with coarse rough hair and the legs are short. As it is a weak flier it allows itself to be driven by the wind like a dead leaf. In rainy weather it lays its fore wings over its hind wings in such a way that the distinctive red marks on the hind wings are hidden. The stages of its life history, the egg, larva and pupa, are unknown.

MORPHO ANAXIBIA ♀

Distribution: *Tropical South America.* Belongs to the Morphid family. The males are of a brilliant blue colour with a faint purple reflection. The wings of the females are more rounded in outline and have a red-gold margin. The undersides of the wings are brown with scattered eye-spots. This colouration forms an effective camouflage for the butterfly when it is resting in the thickets.

HELICONIUS DORIS TRANSIENS

Distribution: *Tropical South America, Colombia to Mexico.* Belongs to the Heliconids. Heliconius doris occurs in three conspicuously different varieties, in both sexes, with occasional intermediates which prove their interrelation. Form transiens is the variety with red hindwing markings. In form viridis the red is replaced by green. In typical doris they are blue.

NESSAEA OBRINUS, *underside*

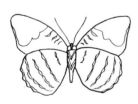

Distribution: *Brazil.* The upperside of the wings is grey-brown in colour with a bluish green band. The colour and markings of the underside form an effective camouflage for the butterfly when it is at rest among the foliage. H. W. Bates says of this species 'This charming butterfly frequents swampy places in the woods of Para and . . . is less often found in the whole Amazon Valley. Its flight is extremely impetuous, but it is fond of resting on leaves where a ray of sunshine breaks through the shade'.

CHARAXES AMELIAE

Distribution: *West Africa.* Belongs to the Nymphalids. The strong wing musculature enables it to fly fast and fearlessly. It visits flowers for the nectar but may also be found on sap flowing from trees and even on various kinds of evil-smelling substances. The caterpillars have two forked processes behind the head; the short stout pupa hangs head down, suspended by its anal hooks.

Plate 7

ORNITHOPTERA PARADISEA

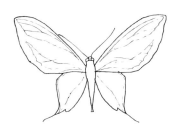

The Paradise Bird-wing Butterfly

Distribution: *New Guinea.* This butterfly, which belongs to the Papilionids, is placed in the genus Ornithoptera (the Birdwinged Butterflies) because of its resemblance to a bird in flight. It is to be distinguished by its magnificent colour and fabulous shape. Paradisea, and the even rarer species meridionalis, are the only Ornithoptera with tailed hind wings. The velvety-black larvae have yellow spines on the body and a yellow forked process behind the head. The unusual angular pupae do not hang on the food plant, but may be found near the ground on low shrubs. The females are black and white and lack tails on the hind wings (sexual dimorphism). This giant butterfly is found in certain areas in the hilly regions and on the coast of New Guinea.

DRURYA ANTIMACHUS

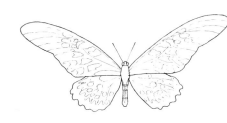

Distribution: *Rain forest regions in tropical Africa.* This is the largest African Papilio species. The leading edge of the long narrow wings is specially strengthened, enabling this gigantic butterfly to glide gracefully above the tree-tops. It is very shy and only alights on the ground to drink water. A collecting expedition (the late Lord Rothschild's) searched unavailingly for the female until a young native produced a 'scrabbling' object. This turned out to be a male and female Drurya antimachus in copula. Both specimens were damaged, but this was the first female to be found. The female is much smaller than the male and the wings are less elegantly shaped.

Plate 8

EPIPHORA BAUHINIAE

Distribution: *South Africa.* Belongs to the Saturnids. The antennae of the males are more pectinate (comb-like) than those of the female. The caterpillar feeds on Zizyphus. It is green and bears tubercles which are red beneath and blue above. The claspers are also red and blue. It spins a large rather thin cocoon.

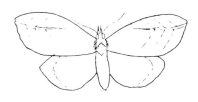

PHYLLODES SPECIES

Distribution: *Eastern India.* This night-flying species belongs to the Noctuidae. When at rest the fore wings are held roof-like over the hind wings. The fore wings are the colour of dead leaves and are of considerable protective value as they make the moth difficult to find among leaves. If an enemy should, however, attack it, it spreads its fore wings, displaying the brilliant warning colours of the hind wings. Another species of this genus is illustrated on plate 25.

CASTNIA HELICONIDES

Distribution: *Tropical South America.* This species belongs to the Castniidae which form an intermediate family between the day and night-flying moths. Most of them are large with thick bodies and strong wings which enable them to fly very fast. The wings are covered with exceptionally large scales. The males are extremely quarrelsome amongst themselves and will attack other moths and even birds in an attempt to drive them away. The eggs of the Castnids are very large compared to those of other moths. The caterpillars live in the roots and stems of bananas, orchids and other plants and specimens often arrive with imported plants; the adult moths sometimes emerge in Europe.

Plate 9

PAPILIO WEISKEI, The Purple-Spotted Swallowtail

Distribution: *New Guinea.* This is one of the most attractive Papilionids.

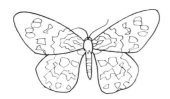

DYSPHANIA MILITARIS

Distribution: *India, Java, Borneo, Halmahera.* Belongs to the Geometrids. The moths of the genus Dysphania are evidently distasteful, as they flaunt their bright colours in broad daylight, visiting the same bushes as sun loving butterflies like the Swallowtails and Whites (Pieridae). The Caterpillar, though a true 'looper' also sits openly on its foodplant though devoid of the camouflage common to most loopers.

ERIBOEA DELPHIS, The Jewelled Nawab

Distribution: *Assam to Java and the Philippine Islands.* Belongs to the Charaxes group. The members of this group are medium-sized butterflies with powerful wings which enable them to fly very fast. The front edge of the forewings is serrate, i. e. bears a series of tiny toothlike projections, a most unusual feature in a butterfly. The hind wings usually have two small tails. Many of these butterflies when caught beat themselves to pieces against the net. The larvae bear at the back of the rather flattened head a pair of horns which project backwards rather like the antlers of a stag.

PAPILIO AEGEUS ♀, The Orchard Swallowtail

Distribution: *New South Wales, Queensland.* Belongs to the Papilionidae, or Swallowtails. The male is dark-coloured (sexual dimorphism). It flies in gardens and open woods. Papilio aegeus also flies in New Guinea and most of the surrounding islands.

Plate 10

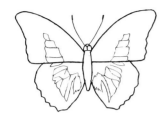

PREPONA PROSCHION

Distribution: *Brazil, Rio Grande do Sul.* Belongs to the Nymphalid genus Prepona. The uppersides of the wings of most of the species belonging to this genus are blackish-brown with a blue band. The species can be distinguished from one another only by the colour and markings of the undersides of the wings. Proschion is considered to be one of the 'better' species because of the rich ornamentation on the underside of the wings.

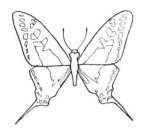

PAPILIO THYASTES MARCHANDII

Distribution: *Mexico to Honduras and Guatemala.* True Papilio thyastes is only found in southern Brazil. Other varieties (subspecies) fly in intermediate regions. In Guatemala thyastes is fairly common up to 2,500 feet above sea level. Papilio thyastes belongs to the section of the genus Papilio characterised by their gliding flight and known popularly as the Kite Swallowtails. Nothing is known of the life history of this species.

PAPILIO TROILUS

The Green-Clouded, Green-Spotted or Spicebush Swallowtail

Distribution: A common butterfly in eastern Canada and extending through the Atlantic states of the U.S.A. to Florida and Texas. A conspicuous visitor to flowers. The caterpillar feeds on spice bush and sassafras within a tube formed by bending the edge of the leaf over to the midrib. A close relative of the common European Swallowtail.

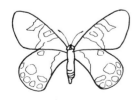

PARNASSIUS CHARLTONIUS, The Red Apollo

Distribution: *Central Asia.* Belongs to the Parnassids, the Apollos. The wings of this species are very lavishly decorated with red eye-spots. They sail elegantly over sunny gorges and rocks and in bright sunlight may be seen sitting with wings outspread on warm rocks.

Plate 11

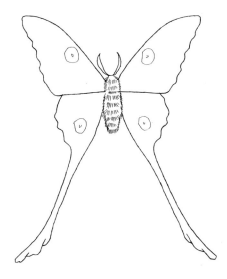

ARGEMA MITTREI

Distribution: *Madagascar.* Flies at the southern end of the island near the Indian Ocean. The specimen depicted emerged from an imported cocoon on August 10, 1954. This is the biggest Saturnid with tailed hind wings. The females are stouter than the males and have shorter tails on the hind wings. The perfect moth usually emerges at night from a silver-filigree-like cocoon, which is, however, very strong. These moths smell very strongly of Bovistid fungi. Fredrick Schnack devotes a whole chapter to this beautiful moth in his book on Madagascar. Dr Diehl, who was for many years a Medical Inspector in Madagascar, has sent many live cocoons to collectors and although moths have emerged from them it has not yet proved possible to breed them in Europe.

ANCYLURIS FORMOSISSIMA

Distribution: *Peru.* Its sparkling colours make this one of the most beautiful butterflies in the world; its specific name is very appropriate. The genus Ancyluris belongs to the Riodinidae, a family closely related to the Blues (Lycaenidae) and having its headquarters in South America, where several hundred species occur, many of them extremely beautiful. In Great Britain there is only one species, the Duke of Burgundy Fritillary.

CRICULA TRIFENESTRATA

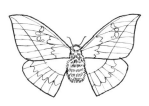

Distribution: *India and Ceylon to Java and the Philippine Islands.* Belongs to the Saturnids. The caterpillar is rather like that of the European Oak Eggar Moth and feeds on the foliage of a wide variety of trees, including Prunus. Every year cocoons from which the adult moths emerge are imported into Europe and it has even proved possible to rear the larvae there.

Plate 12

MORPHO CYPRIS ♀ *FORM:* cyanites

Distribution: *Colombia.* Belongs to the Morphid family. The male (Plate 15) is a beautiful rich blue colour (produced by the breaking-up of the light rays by air-spaces in the wing scales) with yellow and pinkish-violet reflections. The females are usually yellowish-brown. Cyanites is a rare aberrant form.

HEBOMOIA GLAUCIPPE, The Great Orange Tip

Distribution: *from India and China throughout the East Indies almost to New Guinea.* This is the biggest Asian species of the Pierids, which include the 'Whites' and 'Yellows'. In the morning it may be seen flying along paths, at the edges of woods and in clearings. Towards midday it settles down to rest on damp paths. In many of the islands which H. glaucippe inhabits it has developed varieties (subspecies) peculiar to those islands, and it also occurs in dry and wet season forms where there are marked wet and dry seasons.

PAPILIO CLYTIA, The Common Mime

Distribution: *India and Ceylon to China and Singapore, Philippine and Lesser Sunda Islands.* Not present in Sumatra, Java or Borneo. In this Swallowtail the sexes are quite dissimilar, and both are very variable. They are mimics of various species of distasteful butterflies of the genera Danaus and Euploea in whose company they fly, so gaining a measure of protection by deceit. They even copy the slow carefree flight of their models, except when attacked. Essentially a butterfly of the plains, P. clytia is seldom seen above 3000 to 4000 ft. in the hills. It is a common insect easily taken drinking at puddles or feeding at flowers. The caterpillar feeds on various species of Laurineae. The butterfly illustrated on the plate is a variety confined to the Andaman Islands, known as form flavolimbatus. Many other varieties have been described from other places within the range of the species, but few are restricted to particular areas.

78

Plate 13

MORPHO CRAMERI

Distribution: *Brazil and the Amazon basin to Colombia and Guiana.* Better known by its synonym *Morpho perseus.* For hours on end they sail around the tree-tops, very rarely alighting on the ground. The females do not often fly but sit in the undergrowth. The decorated margins of the hind wings distinguish the females from the males.

ORNITHOPTERA BROOKIANA
Rajah Brooke's Birdwing Butterfly

Distribution: *Borneo and Sumatra.* Belongs to the Papilionids, the Swallowtails, although the hind wings lack tails. A special genus, the Ornithoptera, so called because of the bird-like size of these huge butterflies, was established for these Swallowtails of the Indo-Australian region. The species included in this genus are very highly prized by collectors. Brookiana and the very rare species Trojanus, which looks similar but is much larger, are the most beautiful species of the whole group. The broad emerald-green zig-zag band on the velvet-black wings is of indescribable beauty. The males can often be seen drinking along the banks of streams, especially where the path has been fouled by urine. The female, which is very much rarer, prefers to fly high around the tops of flowering trees. Although known to science for over a hundred years, and much prized by collectors, nobody has yet succeeded in rearing this Birdwing in captivity. Not even the food plant of the caterpillar is known for certain.

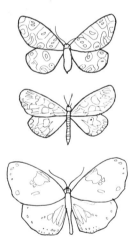

PANTHEROIDES PARDALIS

Distribution: *Brazil.* Nothing is known of the life history of this species.

LONGICELLA MOLLIS DECIPIENS

Distribution: *The Indo-Australian region.* Belongs to the Agaristidae, a family of day-flying moths closely related to the nocturnal Noctuidae.

EUPLOEA DIOCLETIANUS, The Magpie Crow

Distribution: *N. India to Siam, Malaya, Sumatra, Java and Borneo.* An eager flower visitor with a carefree flight; belongs to the large Danaid family. They are avoided by birds because they are distasteful. Illustrated: a male. The female lacks the blue flush.

NEOCHERA BUTLERI

Distribution: *India.* Belongs to the Arctiidae, or Tiger Moths. Butleri is a race of Neochera dominia, which ranges from India to New Guinea and in many places is very common and on the wing all the year round.

Plate 14

METAMORPHO DIDO

Distribution: *Southern Brazil, Honduras, Peru.* Belongs to the Heliconids. This species has a very elegant flight, preferring open clearings in the forest. The emerald-green colouration forms an effective camouflage when the butterfly is resting among leaves. The caterpillar feeds on Passiflora.

SAMIA CYNTHIA, The Cynthia Moth or Eri Silk Moth

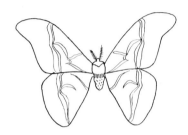

Distribution: *India.* This is one of the Saturnid silk-moths. It is also known as Philosamia cynthia and sometimes as Attacus ricini. The caterpillar, which feeds on Ailanthus glandulosus, the Tree of Heaven, and a great many other trees, is greenish-white in colour and has numerous fleshy protruberances on the body. There are two generations in a year; one hibernates in the pupal stage in a thick yellow-grey cocoon. This moth has been sucessfully introduced into France, Italy, Austria and America. It is in fact such a popular species with collectors who specialise in the Silk Moths that it is now virtually domesticated. It has proved possible to spin and weave the silk which is known as 'Eri silk'.

COLOTIS EUPOMPE

Distribution: *Africa.* One of the 'Whites'. All the species in this group are small or medium-sized butterflies. The headquarters of the genus Colotis are in Africa, but a few species occur also in the near and middle East. Most of the species display marked seasonal dimorphism, especially in the females, most of which lack the conspicuous red patch at the apex of the male's forewing. The larvae feed on Capparidaceae.

EUCYANE BICOLOR

Distribution: *Tropical South America.* This species belongs to the Arctiid family which includes the 'Tiger', 'Ermine' and 'Footman' moths. They fly by day and night and eagerly visit flowers.

COLAENIS STUPENDA

Distribution: *Panama.* C. stupenda is the Panama race of Colaenis phaetusa which ranges thence southward to Peru and Argentina. This species inhabits moist lowlands and has a rather slow flight. The wings remain spread when the insect alights on a flower.

Plate 15

MORPHO CYPRIS ♂

Distribution: *Colombia.* This species is found near the emerald mines of Muzzo and also in the forested river valleys. All the Morpho species are beautiful but this is considered to be the most beautiful of them all. The blue colouration of the wings is produced by the scattering of the light by air-spaces in the wing scales, which are yellowish-brown; in the females there are no air-spaces and therefore the wings remain yellowish-brown in colour. The females sit in the undergrowth awaiting the males which sail around the tree-tops. Blue females (see Plate 12) are very rarely found and are eagerly sought by collectors.

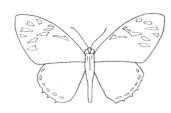

PAPILIO ZAGREUS

Distribution: *Brazil, Bolivia, Venezuela.* Though this species has no tails to the hind wings, it is nevertheless a true Papilio and belongs to the group known as Fluted Swallowtails, owing to the shape of the margin of the hind wing that lies against the body. Its very unusual colour and pattern is due to its being a member of a mimetic Mullerian association (see Introduction, p. 22).

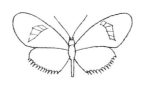

HELICONIUS CYRBIA

Distribution: *Peru, Bolivia, Guiana.* This is one of the more delicately coloured of the species of this remarkable genus, so characteristic of tropical America. Polymorphism (see Introduction, p. 14) runs riot in Heliconius to such an extent that it has so far proved impossible to define the limits of most of the species. Only of recent years are breeding experiments beginning to clarify the situation. All the species are denizens of forest clearings.

Plate 16

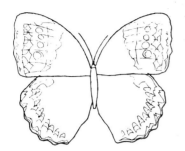

STICHOPHTHALMA CAMADEVA, *upperside*   The Northern Jungle Queen

Distribution: *Sikkim.* This species belongs to the family Amathusiidae. They are closely related to, but morphologically distinct from, the beautiful Morphidae of South America. Camadeva is one of the loveliest of the species of the genus. The Stichophthalma species are large powerful butterflies. From May to September they fly near the ground among the dense vegetation. They are butterflies of the forested hilly country and both sexes are said to emit a strong scent 'resembling that of fresh sable skins'.

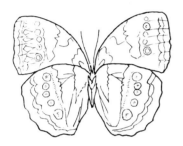

STICHOPHTHALMA CAMADEVA, *underside*

The undersides of the wings are decorated with spots and wavy lines, the pattern forming an effective camouflage which assists the butterfly in escaping detection by its enemies when it is at rest with its wings folded together.

Plate 17

MORPHO AEGA ♀ *YELLOW FORM*

Distribution: *Brazil*. This is one of the smallest but one of the most beautifully coloured Morpho species. The wings of the male are a fine iridescent blue. This colour effect is produced by the breaking up of the light rays by air-spaces in the wing scales. There are no air-spaces in the wing scales of the female, and the wings, as may be seen in the plate, are of a plain yellowish-brown colour. The undersides of the wings of both sexes are of greyish-yellow with a few scattered spots. This colouration forms an efficient camouflage when the butterfly is at rest with closed wings, and thus helps it to escape from its enemies.

MORPHO AEGA ♀ *BLUE FORM:* pseudocypris

Some females have air-spaces in the wing scales; the wings of these specimens are blue but the colour is not as bright as that of the males. Because this form resembles Morpho cypris it is called pseudocypris.

MORPHO AEGA *GYNANDROMORPH*

A caprice of nature; one fore wing is of the bright blue colour of the male, the other the yellow of the female. This is a very rare phenomenon of which very few examples are known.

KALLIMA INACHUS, The Orange Oakleaf Butterfly

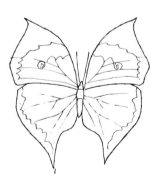

Distribution: *India, Kashmir, Burma, Tonkin, Western and Southern China.* This is one of the Leaf Butterflies; they are remarkable on account of the extraordinary resemblance to leaves exhibited by the underside of the closed wings; even the ribs and stems are represented. It is very difficult to distinguish the butterfly when it is at rest amongst dead leaves. This type of colouration is known as Protective Resemblance. The disappearing trick of this butterfly was well described by A. R. Wallace in a passage which is quoted in the Introduction (p. 20). The butterflies, which may be found on over-ripe bananas, flowering trees and in damp places, fly during the monsoon period; they are not found above 5,000 feet.

88

Plate 18

PAPILIO CRASSUS

Distribution: *Tropical South America, Costa Rica to Rio de Janeiro.* This species belongs to the section of the family Papilionidae known as the Aristolochia Swallow-tails, because all their caterpillars (so far as known) feed on plants belonging to the Aristolochiaceae which are bitter and often poisonous. The butterflies seem to gain some protection in this way as they are mostly regarded as being distasteful. They have long narrow wings which enable them to fly very elegantly.

HYPOLIMNAS DEXITHEA

Distribution: *Madagascar.* Belongs to the Nymphalidae. Many species belonging to the genus Hypolimnas are found in the Indo-Australian region and in Africa. Dexithea is one of the most beautiful of the Hypolimnas species. The males are very quarrelsome. This magnificent butterfly, which is of a rare species, is found in the wooded regions in the northern and eastern parts of the island. Unlike most species of the genus (see Plates 23, 29) H. dexithea is not sexually dimorphic; the males and females are exactly alike in appearance.

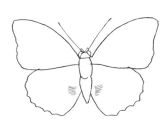

AGRIAS SARDANAPALUS

Distribution: *Tropical South America.* This species belongs to the Nymphalid genus Agrias and ranks among the most beautiful butterflies in the world. Collectors find them very difficult to catch because they are powerful and adroit fliers. The males have a scent-apparatus, in the form of a hair-tuft on the hind wings, which produces an odour that is attractive to the female. The underside of the wings has the appearance of an intricate piece of embroidery (Plate 29). Some specimens of this species have changed hands at very high prices. The species of the genus *Agrias,* like those of the genus *Heliconius,* are so variable that it has not yet been possible to define their real limits. Many which are at present called species will no doubt prove ultimately to be only varieties.

Plate 19

SALASSA LOLA

Distribution: *Eastern Himalayas, India.* The antennae of the males are more pectinate (comb-like) than those of the female. The larvae, which are covered with spine-bearing warts, spin loose cocoons between twigs and leaves on the ground.

MORPHO CATENARIUS ♀ *FORM:* marmorata

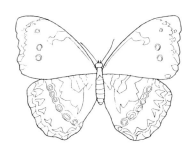

Morpho catenarius (♀ form marmorata) belongs to the Morphids. The brilliant blue of the wings of these species rivals the colour of the sky. The members of the hecuba, perseus and hercules groups have brown wings. The laertes group, to which this species belongs, has pale wings with pearly and opalescent reflections. The underside is decorated with delicate ringshaped markings. The upper surface of the wings of the marmorata form of the female have a marbled appearance. This species is found throughout central South America (Argentine and Brazil). The caterpillars congregate in large numbers on the lianas in the forests. The pupae, which are very plump, hang head down like green berries.

AGERONIA ARETHUSA ♀

Distribution: *South America, Brazil, Peru.* Belongs to the Nymphalidae. In flight the wings produce a strange sound reminiscent of the crackling of stiff paper. Precisely how this sound is produced is not fully understood. On account of it the species of Ageronia are known as Click Butterflies. They are found in the clearings in virgin forests.

CATONEPHELE NUMILA

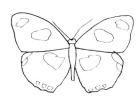

Distribution: *South America, Brazil, Bolivia, Peru.* The specimen illustrated is a male; the very different females have a pale yellow band on the hind wings, and the margins of the wings are of the same colour. This species flies in the densest parts of the forests, but is less attracted to the moisture of brooks and rivulets than to the rotting refuse of the filthiest kinds so common around native huts.

92

Plate 20

PROTAMBULYX EURYCLES

Distribution: *Brazil, Colombia*. Belongs to the Sphingids. The family has been given this name because of a fanciful resemblance which the larvae bear, while at rest, to the Sphinxes of the Egyptian desert. The strong narrow wings enable them to fly very fast. When the moth hovers over a flower, using its long proboscis to reach the nectar, the wings produce a buzzing sound rather like a small motor. The larva has a horn-like spine at the tail. At the end of the larval stage, the caterpillar burrows into the earth where it transforms into a pupa.

ALCIDIS AURORA

Distribution: *New Guinea and several other smaller islands in the same region.* This handsome insect belongs to the Uraniidae which, though moths, habitually fly in the sunshine. A number of very fine species are included in this family. This moth flies above small streams, often in company with Papilio laglaizei which mimics it. The body fluids of Alcidis aurora are distasteful, and for this reason birds avoid it; the mimic is able to profit from this.

BRAHMAEA JAPONICA

Distribution: *Asia, Japan*. This moth belongs to the Brahmaeids. The caterpillars bear very long branching spines upon their bodies, which give them a rather grotesque appearance.

Plate 21

PAPILIO COLUMBUS

Distribution: *Cuba.* This Swallowtail Butterfly belongs to the Aristolochia group of Papilionidae (see Papilio crassus, Plate 18) but is of a more normal shape. It is known only from Cuba where it is fairly common in the hilly eastern districts. It is one of the most beautifully coloured of South American butterflies. It likes to drink from puddles on the ground.

HELICONIUS CHESTERTONI

Distribution: *Peru, Bolivia.* This species is generally regarded as a race of Heliconius hydara which ranges from Costa Rica southwards to Peru. The brilliant yellow band on the hind wing is repeated in several other species in the genus. Due to its long body and narrow wings it is said when in flight to resemble a dragonfly.

HELICONIUS VALA

Distribution: *Guiana.* This species may be seen flying around flowering shrubs together with many other Heliconids. It is one of the numerous forms of another of the excessively variable species of this genus, so typical of the S. American forests, namely Heliconius xanthocles, which ranges from Guiana to Ecuador and Peru (see also plate 15).

CITHERONIA BRISSOTTII

Distribution: *South America.* Belongs to the Saturnids. The interesting larvae which hatch from the large green eggs bear long branching spines upon their backs; these spines are at first longer than the larva itself, but later on when the larva has grown they appear smaller in comparison with the size of the body. The natives call them 'Spiny Devils'. The larva burrows into the earth where it forms a small cell in which it pupates.

PAPILIO DARDANUS ♀
The African Mocker Swallowtail

Distribution: *Africa, S. of the Sahara, Abyssinia, Madagascar.* The wings of the male (♂) are pale yellow with black spots, and the hindwings are tailed. The females are tailless, except in Madagascar and sometimes in Abyssinia. They occur in three principal forms, all of which are excellent mimics of distasteful Danaid butterflies with which they fly. The hippocoon form (illustrated) is a mimic of Amauris niavius; the darker, spotted form cenea mimics Amauris echeria; and the red trophonius form mimics Danaus chrysippus the species mimicked also by the female form of Hypolimnas misippus (plate 23). There are also many intermediate varieties.

Plate 22

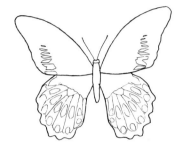

PAPILIO POLYMNESTOR, The Blue Mormon

Distribution: *Ceylon, Southern India to Calcutta.* This species belongs to the Papilionids. They have an elegant flight and may sometimes be seen in the gardens of houses. They usually fly over flat open country, but may occasionally penetrate into hilly regions. They open and close their wings while they feed on flower nectar. The caterpillar is green in colour with a thick thorax; it feeds on citrus plants. The pupa has a silken girdle around the middle of the body.

COPAXA LAVENDERA

Distribution: *Central America, Mexico.* Belongs to the Saturnids. The wings of the male are more curved in outline than those of the female, and the antennae more pectinate (comb-like). The pupae are often sent to collectors in Europe. It is possible to breed this species in Europe as the larvae will feed on the foliage of oak, and sometimes on willow.

THECLA CORONATA

Distribution: *Guatamala, Colombia, Ecuador.* One of the most beautiful of the blue-coloured species with tailed hind wings. The female has a red mark on each hind wing. The underside is almost more attractive than the upper side, being golden-green with a pattern of grey, red and black. T. coronata is one of the very numerous S. American Hairstreak butterflies belonging to the family Lycaenidae, the Blues.

Plate 23

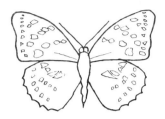

SASAKIA CHARONDA ♂

Distribution: *Japan, North Island to Kiushu.* Belongs to the Nymphalidae, to which the British Purple Emperor (Apatura iris) also belongs. The female is much bigger than the male and lacks its blue gloss. A rare insect, but represented also in Central and W. China by very similar subspecies.

APPIAS NERO ZARINDA, The Orange Albatross

Distribution: *Celebes.* Other subspecies of *Appias nero* are distributed from India throughout the East Indies to Ceram. They belong to the Pierid family which includes the 'Whites' and the 'Yellows'. These butterflies have a strong erratic flight and are often found in damp places such as the edges of pools and puddles and more rarely on flowers.

HYPOLIMNAS MISIPPUS ♀, The Danaid Eggfly

Distribution: *The Indo-Australian region throughout Africa and in North, Central and South America.* The female illustrated is an exceedingly good mimic of the common and very distasteful Danaid butterfly, Danaus chrysippus, the Plain Tiger, which has much the same range. There are also two other forms of the female, each a copy of corresponding varieties of D. chrysippus. The female is sluggish in flight, like the Danaids it mimics. The male, however, flies fast, is black with large blue-flushed white patches on all four wings, and is in no way protectively coloured (see Introduction p. 21). The caterpillar is black with a red head and legs and several rows of branched spines. It feeds on Portulaca oleracea.

PAPILIO CODRUS MEDON, The Silky Swallowtail

Distribution: *New Guinea and the Islands of Waigu, Jobi, Mafor, Biak, and Woodlark.* This is one of the most beautiful of the Swallowtail butterflies. It is swift and strong on the wing, mostly high among tree tops, but can be caught by baiting with rotten fruit, or when drinking at damp sand. Papilio codrus also flies in a number of other East Indian islands between the Philippines and the Solomon Islands.

Plate 24

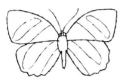

CATAGRAMMA ASTARTE

Distribution: *Bolivia.* This is the Bolivian subspecies of Catagramma codomanus which ranges from Colombia southwards to Brazil, in hilly country rather than in the plains of the Amazon basin. All the species of Catagramma are remarkable for the bold geometrical patterns, in black, blue, yellow or red, of the undersides of their hind wings (see plates 26 and 28).

ATTACUS ATLAS SYLHETICUS, The Atlas Moth

Distribution: *India, in the foothills of the Himalaya Mountains.* This species, which belongs to the Saturnids, is one of the biggest moths in the world. The wings of the female are rather more rounded in outline than those of the male. The enormous caterpillars spin fine webs between the leaves and it is here that they pupate. 'Atlas' silk has been spun from these webs. Cocoons have been sent to Europe and America so that collectors might see for themselves the emergence of this beautiful moth.

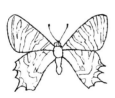

LUEHDORFIA PUZILOI

Distribution: *Eastern Asia.* This species belongs to the Papilionids, the Swallowtails. They are active fliers. The larva spins a silken girdle around its body and then casts off the larval skin. A whole book has recently been published in Japan on the life history of this rather aberrant Swallowtail Butterfly.

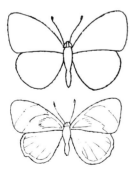

CALLITHEA SAPPHIRA ♂   CALLITHEA SAPPHIRA ♀

Distribution: *Brazil.* The male with its brilliant glowing colours is one of the most beautiful of South American butterflies. It flies in the forests of the Amazon basin. The female may be recognized by the yellow bands on the wings. The undersides of the wings are a delicate green decorated with black spots. The antennae are clubbed. This butterfly exudes a faint odour of vanilla.

Plate 25

PHYLLODES VERHUELLI

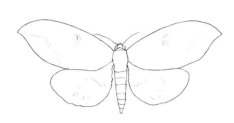

Distribution: *S. E. Asia and the East Indies.* This is one of the Noctuids, and belongs to the Catocalinae, the subfamily which also contains the European Red Underwing Moths. Another handsome species of this genus is figured on Plate 8. The upper surface of the fore wings have the colour and markings of dead leaves. When the moth is at rest the fore wings fold back and hide the brilliantly coloured hind wings, so that the moth is almost indistinguishable from the leaves amongst which it is resting. If, however, the moth is disturbed it spreads its fore wings and displays the warning colouration of the hind wings.

COCYTODES COERULEA

Distribution: *The paleartic regions of Amur, Central and West China.* This species belongs to the Catocalinae, a subfamily of the Noctuidae to which like Phyllodes verhuelli (above) the common European Red Underwings also belong. They have a fast darting flight. The name coerulea refers to the blue bands on the hind wings.

ACHERONTIA ATROPOS, The Death's-Head Hawk Moth

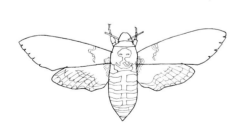

Distribution: *North Africa, Southern Europe.* The Death's-Head Hawk Moth reaches the British Isles annually as a migrant, but does not survive the winter. It belongs to the Sphingids. The family has been given this name because of a fanciful resemblance which the larvae bear, while at rest, to the Sphinxes of the Egyptian desert. They are known to steal honey from beehives. The strong narrow wings enable them to fly very fast and they are able to cover very great distances in a single night. The female often lays her eggs on potato plants or other Solanaceae, such as woody nightshade, on which the larvae feed. The larvae have a crumpled horn at the tail-end of the body. The larva burrows into the ground up to a depth of two and a half inches, and then forms a cell in which it pupates. The moth is able to emit a shrill squeaking sound.

Plate 26

PRECIS RHADAMA

Distribution: *Madagascar*. Belongs to the Nymphalids. Species belonging to the genus Precis also occur in tropical America, Africa and the Indo-Australian region. They contain many examples of startling seasonal dimorphism (see Introduction p. 14).

PRECIS ORITHYA, The Ox-Eyed Pansy

Distribution: *China to Australia and throughout Africa.* This is the most wide-spread of all the species of the genus Precis and the least variable. The only place in which it has developed a sharply defined local race is the oasis of El Hufuf in southern Arabia.

CYMOTHOE SANGARIS

Distribution: *Congo basin to Sierra Leone and Angola.* A member of the Nymphalid family. The underside of the wings has the colour and appearance of dead leaves.

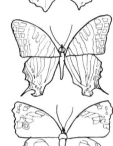

CYRESTIS CAMILLUS

Distribution: *Sierra Leone, Congo Region, Abyssinia.* Although this species has the appearance of a small Swallowtail Butterfly, it belongs to the Nymphalidae.This species has a gliding flight; it settles to rest on the undersides of leaves.

PRECIS CLELIA, The Blue Pansy

Distribution: *Throughout Africa south of the Sahara, and also in Sokotra.* The correct name of this species, which is not very variable, is *Precis oenone*.

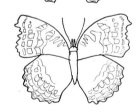

PRECIS OCTAVIA, The Gaudy Commodore

Distribution: *From Natal to West Africa and Abyssinia.* The butterfly illustrated is the dry season form, which is a good deal larger than the wet season form and has a cryptically coloured leaf-like underside. In the wet season form the blue of amestris is entirely replaced by red and the underside pattern is the same as that of the upperside.

CATAGRAMMA PATAZZA

Distribution: *Ecuador, Peru, Bolivia.* The Catagramma species may be regarded as small editions of the much sought after Agrias species. The upper and undersides of the wings of both species resemble one another.

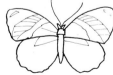

CATAGRAMMA SORANA, *upperside*

Distribution: *Brazil.* Both sides of the wings of these attractive butterflies are magnificently marked and coloured. (Underside Plate 28.)

Plate 27

ORNITHOPTERA HYPOLITUS

Distribution: *Amboina and Ceram in the Indo-Australian region and on the Moluccas and the Celebes.* Although this species lacks tails on the hind wings it is a member of the Papilionid family, the Swallowtails. Because of the large size and bird-like flight of these butterflies they are placed in a separate genus which has been given the name Ornithoptera, which means 'the Bird-wing Butterflies'. Hypolitus is the largest of the yellow and black species. They like to fly along the shore where there are low trees. The life history is quite unknown.

NUDAURELIA ZAMBESINA

Distribution: *East Africa.* This is one of the largest African Saturnid species. This family of moths has been named after the planet Saturn because, like the planet, the spots on the wings have rings round them. The genus Nudaurelia is confined to Africa and contains a large number of species.

Plate 28

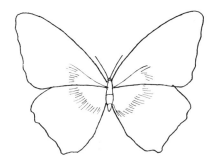

MORPHO HECUBA

Distribution: *Brazil, in the river valleys of the Amazon region.* Belongs to the Morphids; most of the butterflies belonging to this family are blue in colour. Hecuba, which belongs to a yellowish-brown group, is the biggest Morpho butterfly. The undersides of the wings are magnificently decorated with black spots and lines on a silver background, each spot and line being outlined in yellow and black. This species has a very elegant flight and may be seen circling around the tree-tops in the forests.

PHOEBIS AVELLANEDA

Distribution: *Cuba.* This is one of the most beautiful but also one of the rarest of the 'Yellow' butterflies. The species of the genus Phoebis, which are entirely American, were formerly placed in the Old World genus Catopsilia. They are, however, quite distinct. All are notorious visitors to damp patches of sand and to puddles, and many are also well known migrants, flying sometimes in vast swarms.

CATAGRAMMA SORANA, *underside*

Distribution: *Brazil.* The upperside of the wings (Plate 26) is red and black, the underside has the appearance of an intricate piece of embroidery.

PRECIS CEBRENE

Distribution: *Africa.* Precis cebrene is the African subspecies of the Asiatic Precis hierta which is found throughout the hotter parts of India and China. The larva feeds on Acanthaceae and is reddish grey underneath, with small black tubercles on the back and sides.

Plate 29

PARTHENOS SYLVIA TUALENSIS, The Clipper

Distribution: *Key Islands.* This species is a member of the Limenitid group of the Nymphalids, to which the British 'White Admiral' (Limenitis camilla) also belongs. The butterfly illustrated is a local race of Parthenos sylvia, which ranges from India to the Solomon Islands, with many distinct island races (subspecies). They are able to glide effortlessly, only very rarely beating their wings. They are denizens of the lowlands and hills up to 5000 ft. and are usually commonest in the rainy season. The caterpillars feed on vines of the Cucurbitaceae.

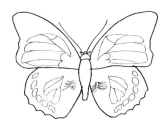

PREPONA PRAENESTE

Distribution: *Peru.* Most of the Prepona species have black or brownish-black wings decorated with a blue band. In addition to the blue reflection, praeneste has purple patches on the wings. They have very strong wing muscles and are able to fly very fast. The males have a scent-producing apparatus in the form of a bunch of hairs on the hind wings. The odour produced by this apparatus is attractive to the female butterfly.

AGRIAS AMYDON, *underside*

Distribution: *The Amazon region.* This genus and the genus Prepona belong to the Nymphalids. With their magnificent colours they rank amongst the most beautiful butterflies in the world and are in great demand by collectors. The male bears a scent apparatus in the form of a tuft of hairs on the hind wings. They are able to fly very fast. (See also Agrias sardanapalus Plate 18.)

HYPOLIMNAS ALIMENA HETEROMORPHA

Distribution: *Key Islands in the Sunda Island region.* This common, fast-flying species belongs to the Nymphalids. The specimen illustrated is the male of a local geographical race of Hypolimnas alimena which inhabits the Moluccan and Papuan subregions in a number of distinct races. There are two principal forms of the female, which is much more variable than the male: one is blue like the male, the other rich warm dark brown, often with much extended white markings. They visit flowers even in the rain, but as they are not at all fastidious they may often be found on evil-smelling substances.

Plate 30

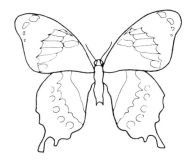

PAPILIO HOMERUS

Distribution: *Jamaica.* Belongs to the fluted section of the Papilionidae, and is the largest American Swallowtail. Papilio homerus flies around the tree-tops and only very rarely alights on the ground. It is restricted to certain localities in the interior of Jamaica and is not common or easy to catch. The caterpillar feeds on Thespesea.

GRAELLSIA ISABELLAE ♀

Distribution: *Central Spain and locally in Southern France.* This is the only European Saturnid species which has tailed hind wings; the wing-tails of the male are longer than those of the female. The caterpillar, found on fir trees, takes three months to reach maturity; it then spins a light airy cocoon among the mosses on the ground. The pupa hibernates and the moth emerges in the spring. The moth flies at night and is attracted to lights.

ERASMIA PULCHELLA

Distribution: *India, Assam.* This magnificently coloured species belongs to the Zygaenids to which the 'Burnets' and 'Foresters' also belong. It is a common species, and its caterpillar, which is velvety black with pale red tubercles, feeds on wild coffee.

MYNES SESTIA

Distribution: *New Guinea.* This is a most attractive butterfly. It is a variety of the widespread species Mynes geoffroyi, which is found throughout New Guinea and the surrounding islands and also in Queensland. It is easily mistaken for a species of Delias (Pieridae) on account of its delicate pastel colouring and the similarity of its flight. It is however a true Nymphalid allied to our European Vanessids. It inhabits lowlands and hills up to 5000 ft., but is never common.

Plate 31

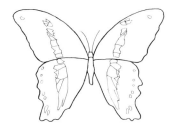

PAPILIO NIREUS, The African Green-Banded Swallowtail

Distribution: *Central Africa.* Belongs to the Papilionids, the Swallowtails, but this species lacks the tails on the hind wings. A number of African species belong to the nireus group. The pupa is very angular.

DANAUS TYTIA, The Chestnut Tiger

Distribution: *India, Himalaya, Assam.* Belongs to the Danaids, the Milkweed Butterflies. The larva feeds on poisonous Aristolochid plants, the juices of which remain active in the body of the butterfly and make it so unpalatable that birds avoid it. These butterflies have a bold carefree flight. Two Papilio species, Papilio agestor and Papilio restrictus, which live in the same region, mimic the markings and flight of this species, thereby gaining protection from their enemies.

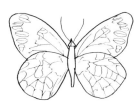

DELIAS HARPALYCE, The Imperial White

Distribution: *India to Australia.* This is one of the 'Whites' belonging to the genus Delias. The undersides of the wings are magnificently coloured, whereas the uppersides are black and white. These butterflies may be found on flowering fruit trees in October, which is one of the spring months in Australia. The caterpillars of Delias harpalyce live gregariously in webs on mistletoe high up near the tops of trees.

PIERELLA NEREIS

Distribution: *Brazil.* Some species belonging to the genus Pierella have transparent patches on the wings. In the closely related South American genera Hetaera and Callitaera the wings are almost entirely devoid of scales and markings except around the outer margin of the hindwing. The characteristic behaviour of these Satyrid butterflies is well described by H. W. Bates (See Introduction, p. 29).

116

Plate 32

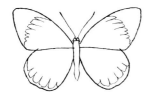

DELIAS AURANTIACA

Distribution: *The volcanic mountains of East Java.* One of the 'Whites'. It is in fact a mountain race of Delias belisama which is much paler. Fruhstorfer relates that it sometimes occurs in such numbers as to rise up like a cloud from the bamboo thickets amongst which it rests. The females, which are much suffused with black on the upper sides, are fond of feeding at the flowers of Cinchona. The undersides of the wings of all the Delias species are beautifully coloured in pastel shades of red, yellow, chocolate and black.

SALETARA OBINA

Distribution: *River banks in the Southern Moluccas.* This species flies very fast. Its bright yellow underside contrasts strongly with the dull leaden colour of the upperside – a most unusual colour in a butterfly.

CHRYSIRIDIA MADAGASCARIENSIS (Urania ripheus)

With its magnificent colours this species ranks among the most beautiful moths. The Uranid family, to which it belongs, includes relatively few species. Urania croesus occurs in *West Africa.* Urania ripheus, which is now known as Chrysiridia madagascariensis, lives in *Madagascar.* The wings are used in the making of butterfly-wing jewellery, and for this purpose thousands of specimens are bred and exported every year. Although this species belongs to a group of night-flying species, it flies by day. They may be seen in the early morning, flying round mango trees and flowering bushes. They drink water very eagerly. (For microphotograph of part of hind wing, see Frontispiece.)

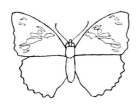

EUTHALIA LUBENTINA, The Gaudy Baron

Distribution: *Northern India and Tonkin to Malaya and the Philippine Islands.* Though said to be fairly common in the hills near Bombay, in most of its range it is a rare butterfly. It likes to feed on flowering trees, but will also feed on decaying fruit. The caterpillar, at least in India, feeds on various species of Loranthus.

DELIAS MYSIS *underside*, The Union Jack

Distribution: *Australia, Papua.* Although the undersides of the wings of the Delias species are very brightly coloured, the upperside is usually white with the margins and angles black. Delias mysis is very common in parts of northern Australia, where its caterpillar feeds on Loranthus.

Plate 33

PAPILIO ULYSSES, The Blue Mountain Swallowtail

Distribution: *New Guinea and neighbouring islands.* Belongs to the Papilionids. Papilio ulysses is possibly the most vivid as well as one of the largest of all the oriental black and blue swallowtails. It ranges over a wide area. The typical form flies in Ambonia and Ceram, islands of the East Indies. From there it is distributed through New Guinea and its neighbouring islands as far afield as the Solomon Islands, most of the island races having their own special names. It flies in woodland and open country with an undulating flight, drinking freely from flowers and damp puddles. The caterpillar feeds on Citrus.

SYKOPHAGES ACHATES

Distribution: *New Guinea, Jobi, Mysore, Waigu, Mysole and Aru Islands.* Better known as *Cyrestis achates.* The species of this genus are well named Map Butterflies. The delicate pattern of wing markings, in spite of its intricacy, is very constant. They fly with a planing flight and settle on the undersides of leaves with the wings spread like a moth — a very unusual habit in a butterfly. The males in particular are much attracted to the moisture of shady forest stream banks. Caterpillars have been found feeding gregariously on the Banyan or Indian Fig Tree.

CATAGRAMMA KOLYMA, *underside*   CATAGRAMMA BROME

Catagramma and Callicore species occur in *Tropical South America.* The upperside of the wings is usually red and black or brilliant blue and black. The pattern on the underside of the wings often resembles the number eighty-eight. Other species of this attractive South American genus are illustrated on Plates 24, 26 and 28.

PAPILIO PAUSANIAS

Distribution: *Tropical South America, Central Colombia, Bolivia, on the Orinoco and Amazon Rivers.* The wings are narrow and lack tails and therefore this species looks more like a Heliconiid species than a Papilionid. It is in fact a very good mimic of Heliconius clytia.

Plate 34

MORPHO HELENA

Distribution: *Peru.* A Morphid. This species resembles Morpho rhetenor in shape and Morpho cypris in colour, and can therefore be called the Rhetenor form of Morpho cypris. With its slender form and beautiful colour this butterfly is entitled to bear the name of the most beautiful woman of the ancient world. The explorer Otto Michael, who accompanied Dr Paul Hahnel on a number of expeditions and afterwards collected for the Staudinger Entomological Institute for many years, gives a very enthusiastic account of the species. It is very rare, and there is scarcely a single museum which possesses a female with the yellowish-brown wings undamaged.

MEGANOSTOMA PHILIPPA, The Dog's-Head Butterfly

Distribution: *Bolivia.* This species belongs to the Pierids; it used to be included in the same genus, Colias, as our Clouded Yellow Butterflies, but is now placed in a separate genus on account of morphological differences. The genus Meganostoma occurs, in a number of species, from the southern United States of America to Argentina.

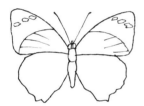

SMYRNA BLOMFILDIA

Distribution: *Tropical America.* This species belongs to the Nymphalids. It has a swift active flight, and, as it is a very common species it is one of the first to be noticed by the visitor to South America. Not confined to forest country only.

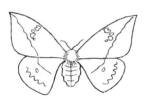

CRICULA ANDREI

Distribution: *India.* Belongs to the Saturnids. Live cocoons often arrive in Europe, where it is possible to rear this species, as the larvae will feed on lilac, vine and willow leaves. The caterpillars are quite unlike those of the other species of Cricula, figured on Plate 11, as they are apple-green and not densely hairy.

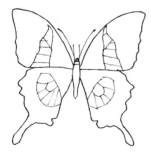

PAPILIO BUDDHA, The Malabar Banded Peacock

Distribution: *Hill Regions of Southern India.* This species belongs to the Palinurus group of the Papilios. It may be seen all the year round, except in June and July, but it is commonest in September and October. It flies very quickly and high. Its green caterpillar feeds on Xanthoxylum rhetsa.

Plate 35

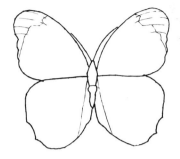

CALIGO BELTRAO, The Owl Butterfly

Distribution: *Central and Southern Brazil.* This species is common in the State of Santo Spiritu. All the species belonging to the genus Caligo are large in size; although they belong to the day-flying butterflies, they appear only at dusk. At other times they sit head-down in the dense undergrowth. The undersides of the wings are marked with large eye-spots. If the butterfly is attacked by an enemy, such as a lizard, the wings suddenly open and the enemy is driven away by a frightening owl-like face.

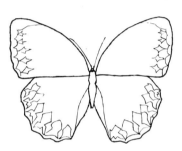

STICHOPHTHALMA HOWQUA

Distribution: *India, Eastern Himalayas, and also Formosa and Western China.* The eastern Amathusiidae do not equal their South American relatives the Morphos in size and brilliance. They are all large butterflies which may be seen on the wing from March to May. The males have a scent-apparatus in the form of a tuft of hairs on the hind wing; the odour produced by this apparatus attracts the females. Only in Western China does this handsome butterfly appear to be moderately common. Elsewhere it is exceedingly rare.

Plate 36

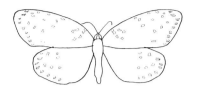

ERASMIA SANGUIFLUA

Distribution: *India, Burma, Sumatra, Java and Borneo.* This species belongs to the Zygaenids, the family to which the British 'Burnets' and 'Foresters' belong. This fast and active day-flying moth is found at altitudes of 3000 to 6000 ft. It is very tenacious of life, being strongly resistant even to cyanide.

JEMADIA HOSPITA, *Form:* ulyxes

Distribution: *South America.* Belongs to the Hesperids, the Skippers. The wings are smaller in proportion to the body than in most butterflies. They are quick to take flight when they are disturbed. Jemadia is one of a number of genera of similarly stout-bodied Skippers peculiar to South America placed in the sub-family Pyrrhopyginae, and containing a number of genera and species grouped in Mullerian mimetic associations (see Introduction p. 22).

THYSONOTIS PHILOSTRATUS

Distribution: *Moluccas.* An attractive butterfly with a very graceful flight. The genus Thysonotis is virtually restricted to the Papuan subregion. Most of the species are beautifully patterned on the underside in white and silver on a black background.

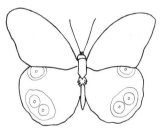

TAENARIS DOMITILLA

Distribution: *Islands in the Indo-Australian region, especially the Moluccas.* All the species included in the genus Taenaris have one or more eye-spots on the hind wings. They all have the same pale grey or brownish mousey colour. They are very variable and difficult to classify. The smoothly green, rather sluggish, caterpillars bear horns on the head and tend to live gregariously on palms.

PAPILIO BRASILIENSIS

Distribution: *Brazil.* This Swallowtail Butterfly belongs to the Thoas group of the Papilios. The caterpillar, which when alarmed protrudes a forked process from behind the head, spins a silken girdle around its body before it pupates. The butterflies have a very elegant gliding flight.

Plate 37

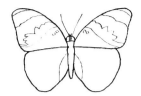

EUPHAEDRA NEOPHRON, The Gold-Banded Forester

Distribution: *Africa, Delagoa Bay to Kenya.* This species belongs to the Nymphalids. Euphaedra neophron is one of the few species in this genus to display very little variation, either individually or geographically (see E. eleus, below).

HENIOCHA MARNOIS

Distribution: *Africa, East and Central Africa.* This species belongs to the Saturnids, and is very reminiscent of the European Emperor Moths.

TEINOPALPUS IMPERIALIS ♂, The Kaiserihind

Distribution: *India, Nepal to Tenasserim, Sikkim, Bhutan, Assam and Northern Burma.* This member of the Papilionid family has powerful wings which enable it to fly very swiftly. It flies in wooded mountainous regions between 6,500 and 10,000 feet, around tree tops from 8 to 11 in the morning, after which it disappears.

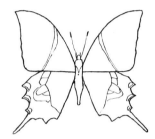

BAEOTUS BAEOTUS

Distribution: *Brazil, in the upper reaches of the Amazon.* Belongs to the Nymphalidae. This species has a fast active flight. On the underside both sexes are alike, but on the upperside the male has a broad blue band, the female a wide brown band, across both wings, against a black background.

EUPHAEDRA ELEUS

Distribution: *Africa, Sierra Leone, Uganda, Congo.* Belongs to the Nymphalids. Quite a large number of African butterfly species belong to this genus. Euphaedra eleus is a much more variable species than E. neophron, figured above, especially in the male sex, which is unusual in butterflies, the females generally being the more variable sex. The reddish brown of the upperside is often replaced by shining green or bluish tones, more rarely by deep chocolate brown.

Plate 38

PARNASSIUS AUTOCRATOR ♀

Only a very few collections possess a specimen of this rare and much sought after butterfly. In 1911 a single specimen was captured at Darwas in Western Pamir. The species remained unknown for almost a quarter of a century until it was rediscovered in 1936 by the adventurous collecting expedition led by the well known entomologist Dr Hans Kotzsch, of Dresden. Dr Kotzsch and his wife, who accompanied him, were able to capture several specimens of both sexes. The males are much rarer than the females; it is the only Apollo Butterfly in which the female has a large yellow spot on the hind wings. These butterflies fly with an elegant sailing motion above rocky gorges and chasms. This specimen was captured in the Chodja-Mohamed mountain range in Afghanistan.

COPIOPTERYX SEMIRAMIS

Distribution: *The forest regions of Brazil, the State of Santo Spiritu and the forests of Venezuela,* where this specimen was captured. This species belongs to the Saturnids. With their long hind-wing tails trailing behind them and their eyes growing golden, these moths glide like ghosts through the forests in the late hours of the night. Nothing is known of their developmental stages. In his book on the Rancho Grande, Bebée describes how a female which had considerably shorter hind wing-tails, flew against the windows of his laboratory in the forest. She laid yellowish-white eggs in a cardboard box and in a fortnight spiny larvae hatched out, but they refused to feed and died within a few days.

THECLA MARSYAS

Distribution: *Panama to South Brazil.* This species is a Hairstreak belonging to the family Lycaenidae. It is a common butterfly throughout its range. The underside is dove-grey with a pinkish tinge, ornamented with small scattered black spots and short lines.

SERICINUS TELAMON KOREANA

Distribution: *Korea.* This pretty butterfly belongs to the Papilionids. It has a very elegant flight. Sericinus telamon ranges from Vladivostok to Shanghai and across to Western China. The subspecies figured, as its name implies, comes from Korea. The butterfly is local, but usually common where it occurs; and its spring and summer broods show noticeable differences. The caterpillars feed on Aristolochia.

TEMENIS LAOTHOE

Distribution: *Mexico, Paraguay, Peru.* This species, which sometimes appears in very large numbers, loves to feed on flowers and to drink water.

130

Plate 39

ORNITHOPTERA PRIAMUS

Distribution: *Papuan subregion (Moluccas to Solomon Islands) and N. E. Australia.*
This species belongs to the Papilionids, the Swallowtails, but it lacks tails on the hind
wings. It is as big as a bird and therefore, together with other similar species, is placed
in a special genus, the Ornithoptera, or Bird-wing Butterflies. The wing colours of the
males of the Priamus differ from island to island – they may be green, golden-yellow, or
blue on a black background. The blue form illustrated is urvillianus, which flies in New
Hanover and the Solomon Islands. The golden-yellow (or orange) form flies in
Halmahera and Batjan. The remaining areas are occupied by the green form, priamus,
but there are also some slight modifications on other islands. The female is always black
and grey or black and white. The males fly around the tops of trees while the females
remain nearer the ground. These butterflies are the first to be noticed by the traveller
who is usually impressed by their size and beauty. The spiky pupae, which have a silken
girdle around the middle, are found on low bushes.

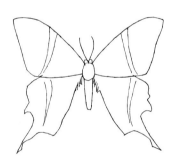

NYCTALEMON ACHILLARIA

Distribution: *Java.* Nyctalemon achillaria is usually regarded as the Javanese subspecies
of Nyctalemon patroclus which has a range from India to the Solomon Islands. It
belongs to the Uraniidae (see Plate 32), many of which mimic Swallowtail Butterflies.
This species, however, is purely nocturnal and its resemblance to a Swallowtail is due
to convergent evolution, not to mimicry. It hides by day, away from the light in native
huts and similar places, with its wings spread flat in the manner of the Geometrid
(Carpet) Moths. The larvae are cylindrical, light to dark brown in colour, with scattered
soft bristles. Before pupating the larvae spin loose cocoons between withered leaves.

INDEX OF SCIENTIFIC AND POPULAR NAMES